To run the Dramarathon you need stamina. In the course of many millennia – at least 300,000 years, by my reckoning, but probably more – you will incarnate as saint and sinner, rich man, poor man, male and female. Your skin will be black, yellow, pink, olive, your nationality anything from Lapp to Turk, Russian to Prussian, Dutch to Polynesian.

You will die in the cradle, in warfare, in comfort and in the geriatric ward. And in between birth and death, you will experience everything – all the pains and joys, triumphs and failures known to humanity. By the end of it all, you'll truly know yourself. . .

Roger Elliot

Who Were You?

A MAYFLOWER BOOK

GRANADA
London Toronto Sydney New York

Published by Granada Publishing Limited in 1981

ISBN 0 583 13442 4

A Granada Paperback Original
Copyright © Roger Elliot 1981

Granada Publishing Limited
Frogmore, St Albans, Herts AL2 2NF
and
3 Upper James Street, London W1R 4BP
866 United Nations Plaza, New York, NY 10017, USA
117 York Street, Sydney, NSW 2000, Australia
100 Skyway Avenue, Rexdale, Ontario, M9W 3A6, Canada
PO Box 84165, Greenside, 2034 Johannesburg, South Africa
61 Beach Road, Auckland, New Zealand

Printed and bound in Great Britain by
Cox & Wyman Ltd, Reading
Phototypesetting by Georgia Origination, Liverpool
Set in Plantin

Granada ®
Granada Publishing ®

TO BEN

whoever he may be

How to Use This Book

This is not your only lifetime on Earth. You have been here many times before, and will keep returning, life after life, until you are a perfect human being.

WHO WERE YOU? is designed to help you discover your past lives. This does not involve hypnosis or clairvoyance or magic. It is based on astrology, the science of the heavens. For you can return to Earth only at the appropriate moment, when Sun, Moon and planets form the right pattern.

This pattern is like a combination lock. Only when the Solar System is correctly set for *your* identity will the door of heaven open and allow you to be born.

Your horoscope is the key to this door of destiny. It tells us your true identity and the journey you've made to get to your present stage of development. It cannot tell us for certain whether you were, say, Marie Antoinette in your last life. But it's still full of fascinating clues to the kind of person you were – the career you followed, the emotional life you led, the good deeds and the wasted chances that have come back to haunt you in this life.

The book splits into two sections, theory and practice. The first half looks at the whole concept of reincarnation, and shows how astrology is linked with it. The second half enables you to analyse your own horoscope and find an answer to the biggest question of all: who *were* you?

THEORY

PRACTICE

CHAPTER ONE

Who Was I?

I was Ben Jonson.

There are three likely responses to this *pronunciamento*. The first is 'Ben *Who*?', which betrays a shocking ignorance of 17th-century English dramatists. The next is a snuckle - the sound, halfway between a snort and a chuckle, that people make whenever they see a fool floating wide-eyed into cloud-cuckoo land. The third response, increasingly·frequent these days, is 'Ben Jonson, eh? That makes sense. Now what about *my* previous lives?'

You'd love to know, wouldn't you? Imagine the joy of gaining access to some celestial computer that could print out - in the twinkling of an eye, without any fuss on your part - a list of your previous identities. Something like this:

ELLIOT ROGER alias Cinna the poet, 1st century BC, Rome
Fung Hao the blacksmith, Tang Dynasty, Peking
Hortha the monk, Dark Ages, Ireland
Marion the Maid, Disneytime, Sherwood Forest

You must admit it's fun. I can picture myself as Fung Hao, hammering the Emperor's armour into shape. But even if this catalogue of past lives were true, it remains utterly trivial. For it turns history into one long gossip column, a chronicle of who wore what at the great fancy-dress party.

This is the terrible charm of reincarnation. It can cater to all our worst instincts. Listen, for a moment, to this snatch of conversation. You could overhear it almost anywhere these days - not simply at spiritual retreats or consciousness-raising sessions but down at the local supermarket. I've set it in the Californian happy hour:

'I was in Greece, you know. I learnt so much in that incarnation.'

'And then Rome. I'm sure we knew each other in Rome.'

'We did, dear. My spirit guide told me. I was your mother in Rome.'

'My *mother*? But my spirit guide said you were my *son*.'

'Maybe your guide had an off-day. All that matters is that we formed deep personal ties.'

'*Karmic* ties.'

'Right, honey. And there's still some heavy karma between us.'

'Do you think so?'

'I know so. I can feel it. That's why I have this deep latent hostility towards you.'

'Oh no. You can't have. Not me.'

'Sure, it goes way back. You were cruel to me in the past.'

'When? In Rome? In Greece?'

'You were *never* in Greece! Pythagoras wouldn't have you. Fix me another drink and I'll tell you about the Inquisition.'

This exchange – imaginary but typical – has all the hallmarks of the popular approach to reincarnation. Note, first of all, the underlying snobbery. These people aren't content to be tribal Africans or peasants in Asia Minor – oh no, they claim always to have lived at the best addresses, in the finest cultures, among the high achievers of all time.

Observe their sources of information. They place great reliance on intuition (their own, at any rate – they're inclined to distrust anyone else's). And they put much faith in one special voice of wisdom: an inner spirit guide, perhaps, or sometimes a medium or teacher whom they know personally, or sometimes a guru whose books they have read. They have no time for science, scepticism or commonsense.

Notice, too, how their past lives are used as weapons in their present-day ones. They take a sublime concept like karma – the Hindu word for the spiritual debts that we carry from one life to the next – and use it to score points off each other. Within occult circles there's a great deal of spiritual in-fighting, with personal dreams and visions and special messages being employed as moral blackmail to gain ascendancy over others.

When you see people willingly dominated by a spiritual bully – and there are many nowadays, masquerading as messiahs – you don't know whether to laugh or cry. Or snuckle.

Which brings us back to Ben Jonson. Trust Roger, I can hear you murmur, to pick a nice, warm-hearted, cuddly old celebrity! None of your Bombay beggars or Aussie aboriginals for him – oh no, he heads straight for the top! And he tries to lecture *us* about claiming famous men as earlier incarnations. Ben Jonson, indeed! What a hypocrite!

Well, I was never really *sure* I was old Jonson. It was my family that believed so. From a greatly respected psychic, Grace Cooke, came the impression over the years that Roger had been...well, some larger-than-life character...active in literature...much admired by the public...someone who had brought great humour and gusto to his work.

Blend these fragments with various guesses, hunches and intuition, and presto! – Roger must be the reincarnation of beloved Ben.

Everything seemed to fit. Hadn't I always been drawn to the swashbuckling Elizabethan era? Wasn't I – like Ben – a natural exhibitionist? Hadn't I always planned to be a writer? And, most telling of all, didn't I share the same warmly cynical, good-natured, worldly-wise attitude to life as portrayed in Jonson's plays? There couldn't be any doubt. I was honest Ben, reborn.

To illustrate the point, my father enjoyed quoting a typical Jonson story. Evidently, at some stage in his life, the dramatist had turned his back on the Church, or, perhaps, been temporarily excommunicated. At all events, when, at last, he was able to take communion again, he was so eager to embrace the faith once more that he snatched the huge silver chalice from the priest and, raising it to his lips, drained all the wine in one long gulp. 'That sounds like Roger!' chuckled Father.

I was not the only historical celebrity in the family. My brother Anthony had been another Elizabethan – Anthony Bacon, no less, the brother of the great philosopher Francis Bacon. In support of this, there was the similarity of names and the fact that both Anthonys were ever-so-slightly sickly, tending to take to their beds with mysterious inner fevers.

More seriously, my family believed that we all had special links with Francis Bacon, a man treasured in our minds as the fount of much wisdom. Those of you familiar with the Baconian Theory will know its main tenets: that Bacon wrote the Shakespeare plays and indeed inspired the whole English literary renaissance; that he founded the Rosicrucian movement; and that he was also the secret child of Queen Elizabeth and the Earl of Dudley – in short, the rightful heir to the throne. Denied this inheritance, he laboured in secret to bring knowledge to the world. My brother Anthony – that is, *his* brother Anthony – acted as a personal secret agent, gathering intelligence from all over Europe. I, meanwhile, was one of his 'good pens', one of a band of anonymous writers who helped him compose the bulk of Elizabethan and Jacobean literature.

My mother, so it was darkly hinted, had been Lady Anne Bacon, the mother (or rather *foster*-mother) of the great Francis himself – and therefore mother then (as now) of both Anthonys. And my father – well, perhaps he was Sir Nicholas Bacon (husband to Lady Anne, alias my mother)...but perhaps, just perhaps, he had been...*Burleigh*, Queen Elizabeth's prime minister!

My sister, who had never got as caught up in the Baconian saga as raptly as the rest of us, was never assigned a part in this particular Elizabethan pageant. Her great moment was 1,500 years earlier, when she was a Vestal Virgin *who broke her vows!*

Around the same time, but in another neck of the woods, my brother-in-law Peter was playing a crucial role as a Roman soldier on a hill just outside Jerusalem. I may well have watched him do the deed, for I had certainly been at the Feeding of the Five Thousand (eating again!) where I had become a Christian. Nice to be in at the start of things.

I recount this family *Who's Who* with mixed feelings. One part of me, still loyal to my upbringing, wants to defend the truth of these assertions. Anyone who has been taught a particular faith, be it religious, political or any other, knows how powerfully it can grip one's consciousness, particularly if the training begins at an early age. Even when one reaches what the Church calls 'the years of discretion', one is hard-pressed to discard childhood beliefs that are, according to one's logical mind, rubbish. Catholics who lapse, for instance, rarely take the final step into atheism. They keep their options open.

Perhaps I share this widespread reluctance to abandon ideas that are part of my upbringing. In addition, though, I have inner evidence that some, at least, of these *dramatis personae* come near to the truth. Such evidence – private, as I say, and perhaps convincing to me alone – should not be used to win converts. But when dreams, meditations or sudden flashes of recognition seem to support what you have been told, you cannot help thinking that your beliefs are being reinforced by personal experience.

Another part of me is much more sceptical. Like most people as they grow older, I have become wary of innocence. I have seen too many fools misled, too many easy answers blandly accepted, too many mountains of dogma washed away by the rainfall of commonsense. And, again like most intelligent people, I've learnt to respect the scientific approach. If proof is needed, then evidence must be sifted and corroborated, shown to be accurate, and rigorously questioned. Ideas must remain hypotheses until all alternative explanations are rejected. Personal hopes and wishes must be set to one side.

This bluff, objective viewpoint has certainly not triumphed
– yet – over my residual faith in reincarnation. Within my
mind there's a constant debate taking place – between heart
and head, belief and knowledge, intuition and regional thought.
It's a debate, of course, that's shared by many people – not
necessarily about reincarnation alone, but about God, miracles,
UFOs, astrology, life after death, and a thousand other metaphysical topics. For many of us, it is the central argument of
our lives: how to reconcile the two different sorts of wisdom
that inhabit our minds.

There are many names for these wisdoms, but, for the sake
of simplicity, let's call them intuition and logic. Some people
believe that the human mind – perhaps through accidental
evolution, or the design of God – is based on dualism. They
maintain that all our philosophy, our art, our religion, our
political and social ideas are based on the interaction of the
intuitive and logical minds. Others, swayed by an over-
emphasis of one of these mentalities, would say that the
other way of thinking was just a delusion. They may be
scientists who reject any kind of inner knowledge; or they may
be spiritualists who discard all logical thinking as though it
were some kind of evil, low-grade manifestation of the Devil.
Our Californian couple, mentioned above, clearly fall into this
category; while all the behaviourists in psychology and
Darwinians in biology are, just as clearly, members of the
opposite camp.

My own desire – shared, I would have thought, by most
reasonable people – is to accept the existence of both mental
disciplines and try to marry them together. I want to find an
explanation of the universe that satisfies both my intuition and
my logical faculties.

Intuition seems the weaker approach altogether. It has no
real means of proving its assertions; it is horribly open to fraud
and self-deception; and throughout the last few centuries it has
been forced to yield ground to its dominant sister, logic. But it

remains the most powerful force possessed by mankind. For all the wonders of modern technology, science has signally failed to disprove *any* intuitive truths. It cannot even say what an inner feeling is; how religious conviction works; why we can be so totally dominated by our chosen beliefs, to the exclusion, at times, of anything else. Science, in other words, is a brilliant means of looking at *certain kinds of experience*; but still surprisingly inept when examining other aspects of life.

Take reincarnation, for instance. Intuition has told the vast majority of Earth's people, going back endlessly into history, that there is a life after death; and a smaller but still considerable majority have believed that they themselves, instead of migrating to a heaven in another universe, return over and over again, in a variety of bodily and temperamental guises, spending many lifetimes on this planet.

Intuition has also told these millions of people that there is a purpose in life – namely, spiritual evolution. Long before the idea of physical evolution was put forward by Darwin, humble tribesmen and villagers throughout the world were accepting the notion of soul development: that each one of them was an individual whose duty, through many lives, was to enhance his qualities so perfectly that he could escape the wheel of rebirth and be reunited with God in seventh heaven, known as *nirvana*.

Now I accept all the *ifs* and *buts* that must properly be attached to these beliefs. Yes, these people were instructed in them from childhood. No, they had no alternative knowledge against which to measure their credo. And yes, they also had superstitions and magical practices that have been totally rejected by even 'intuitive' people today. So why, you may argue, cling to this one particular belief – reincarnation – to the exclusion of the others?

Well, what of the scientific alternative? Current logical thinking would assert that, first, there is no existence for us once our vital organs have ceased to function; and secondly, our development, if you can call it that, is totally based on chance: *short-term* chance, in the sense that our individual lives are shaped by the environment that we happen, quite by accident, to be born into; and *long-term* chance, in that our collective survival as a species is dependent on nothing more than random cellular mutations.

Logic, in other words, gives no real value to what we *feel* within our hearts about our personal destiny. Indeed, it attaches no significance whatever to our existence. We just happen, that's all.

Despite this bleak prognosis, science cannot be ignored. Science asserts that there is absolutely nothing in reincarnation whatsoever. And so, on the flimsy assumption that if logic is stunningly correct in some ways – building space-ships, analysing the atom, curing diseases – it may as well be correct in everything, I allowed its cool, uncaring scepticism to start eroding my belief in reincarnation.

Today I'm suspended midway between belief and dismissal of this ancient doctrine. You might think that sitting on this fence is an awkward posture – certainly a poor starting-point for writing a book on the subject. But I feel that I have reached the most credible position possible. Torn between serious belief and solemn logic, I have opted for a Zen-like third approach. I have turned the whole matter into what may be called a metaphysical game. And I have done so with the help of another such game – astrology.

Metaphysical Games

I use the word *game* in a highly provocative way. For most people, especially those of a religious frame of mind, games are pastimes, amusements with no relevance to the real world. They are an escape from truth. Indeed, for Mr and Mrs Average, the word *game* used in connection with anything 'occult' instantly arouses the suspicion in their minds that they are being hoaxed.

Let me assure them that I don't use *game* in the sense of trick or leisure pursuit, but as an *imaginative model*. Football is an imaginative model of a battle. So is chess, in its own highly stylized way. Grand masters hunched silently over a chequered board seem a far cry from the stench and blood of warfare, but in their minds they are army commanders ordering their troops into action.

They are playing a special version of the universal game, known as Let's Pretend.

Even the most rigorously logical people – scientists – play games. In their case, they are known as mathematical models. They use these models to design bridges, calculate the world population 10,000 years ago, or guess how galaxies are made. They establish certain parameters, which can be called the rules of the game; and then they invent a multitude of ways, called strategies, of playing the game. They pretend to hurl hurricanes or bombs or metal fatigue at their proposed bridge, just to see how well it stands up to the treatment. They pretend that famine, war and disease hit the world in precisely measured doses, just to see how the overall population would be affected. They pretend that different gas clouds have different densities and speeds, just to see what galactic shapes turn up on the computer screen.

Obviously we all know that intuitive people are a good deal more imaginative than that. Painters pretend that the paint on the canvas is a three-dimensional landscape. I pretended – no sorry, *Ben Jonson* pretended that his plays were represent-ations of real life. Very few people actually take him at his word. They obey Aristotle's advice to 'suspend their disbelief' – in other words, they join in the game of Make Believe, knowing that it's only a game. But it's a *serious* game. Nobody leaves the theatre after seeing *The Alchemist* shouting 'I've been hoaxed! Jonson's just a cheap trickster!' On the contrary, he's acclaimed as a great creative artist.

Now we come to the puzzling bit. There is one area in life

where you are not allowed to play games. In religious and metaphysical matters, no imaginary models of any description are permitted. And this is puzzling because, self-evidently to me, religion – or myth-making, if you like – is the one area of human activity where true creative imagination is absolutely *required*. Without it, religion doesn't exist.

Clearly each particular religion requires some kind of imagination, simply to get its message across in the first place. But it's a highly disciplined imagery, almost totalitarian in its control. In this respect, organized religion resembles professional sport. The activities are so drilled and regulated, the training so harsh, the aims so solemn and single-minded, that all the true fun of Let's Pretend is taken away.

What religion and sport won't allow you to do is change the ground-rules. In pro tennis – a very solemn business indeed – you cannot suddenly say 'Let's play three-a-side.' In religion, too, you cannot say 'Let's be Muslims today' or 'Let's pretend that God doesn't exist.' You are bound by the rules, the doctrine.

Of course, things aren't as bad as they once were, when you were excommunicated if, like me – er, Ben – you didn't see eye to eye with the Church authorities. But today's looser discipline is just as invidious, for it involves the same, deep spiritual injunction: *do not lose faith.*

Whereas the artists encourage you to suspend your disbelief, the priests admonish: *disbelieve at your peril.*

What happens at the moment is that children are usually brought up in the faith of their parents and the community around them. In the West, this usually means a sentimental reverence for Jesus and perhaps also Mary. Even if the parents are agnostics, the children still absorb the prevailing religious faith from school and TV. Of course, later on, they may study comparative religion, or they may come into fervent contact with people from another faith. But all too rarely are they encouraged, from an early age, to *create* their own religion, according to their own special psychological pattern.

The Game of Astrology

For myself, over the last fifteen years, this psychological pattern has been revealed - in part, at least - through astrology.

In other words, I believe that the pattern of the planets at your birth is a complex symbol of the pattern of your personality. For some reason, as yet unknown, you are born at the moment that is, according to the heavens, exactly appropriate to the type of psyche that you have.

From this pattern, it's possible to get a remarkably detailed picture of your temperament, inner character, emotional disposition, skills and aptitudes, likes and dislikes - a rounded portrait, in fact, based not on personal observation or psychological tests but purely on this odd-looking diagram full of hieroglyphs, known as your horoscope.

To you, of course, this may all be ridiculous mumbo-jumbo, the sort of fuzzily intuitive practice that should have been left behind in the Middle Ages. If so, I suggest that you read one or two books mentioned in Chapter Twelve, LEARNING MORE - in particular, *Recent Advances in Natal Astrology*, which shows, in great scientific detail, just how much progress has been made in modern astrology. It's a much more logical subject than people realize, akin to modern weather forecasting. In the same way that meteorologists receive reports from various weather stations and, in the light of past experience, make forecasts of how the weather will develop, so do astrologers analyse the horoscope into its component parts and using past experience as a guideline, make predictions about how the person will behave in the years ahead.

Weather forecasting has a wide variety of uses, from the trivial matter of planning your picnic to crucial decision-making in agriculture or marine transport. Astrology, too, can be applied at many levels. It, too, can help to plan the right month for your holiday; but more profoundly, it can look into

your soul, helping you to understand the innermost workings
of your own psyche. This is where astrology operates most
effectively – as a catalyst triggering your own inner self-
knowledge. In the right circumstances, astrological science and
intuition can flow together, producing a wonderful river of
self-discovery back to your true psychological roots.

These roots can be described in many different ways –
Freudian, Christian, behaviourist, anyway you like; but, in
common with many astrologers nowadays, I have found that
astrological ideas marry most happily with Jungian concepts.
The psychological archetypes unearthed by psychologist Carl
Jung in this century bear an uncanny resemblance to the
Zodiacal characteristics known, as part of folklore, for
millennia. Jung's Trickster, for example, is Gemini spot-on;
Mother is Cancer, Father is Capricorn; and so on, round the
heavenly circle of stars. In the same way, Jung's *animus* and
anima correlate closely with the role of Sun and Moon in
astrology.

So it's possible, taking any particular horoscope, to discern
which archetypes will contribute most powerfully to the
development of that person's psyche. All humans have access
to all emotions, of course; but we know perfectly well that
some people are more aggressive than others, some more
spiritual, some more adventurous. It's as though we are cakes
made with differently proportioned ingredients; some of us are
over-egged, others are under-sugared, others have too much
flour or too little icing. Our task, according to Jung and
modern astrological thinkers, is, firstly, to recognize in what
proportions our psychological ingredients are mixed, and,
secondly, to live at peace with this mixture, integrating them
as best we can into a rounded and adult personality.

You can see that astrology is a serious metaphysical game. It
creates a model of the psyche which you can poke, handle, take
apart or expand to your heart's content. There's enough
evidence now to show that there's some *objective* scientific

validity to astrology; and there are certainly enough sensible believers to establish a *subjective intuitive* validity. There is a real truth to it.

In my most rigorously scientific frame of mind, I reject a good deal of religion – and reincarnation, for that matter. Then, on second thoughts, I grant it a sort of second-class citizenship. The gods and goddesses of all religions, according to this view, are not *real*, but embodiments of the underlying archetypes. We worship those archetypes that make the most powerful resonance within our individual nature; and we treat as devils those other archetypes that we fear and despise.

By the same token, if we feel strongly about a historical place or character, this need not necessarily be a sign that we have been associated with that place or character in the past. No, it's simply that they reverberate in tune with psychological needs of our own. For my family, Francis Bacon embodies a potent archetype: the Wise One, the omniscient figure who can impose intellectual order on chaotic experience. Ben Jonson, meanwhile, embodies what is called a *sub-personality* in my own psyche: a projection of myself in what I, and people who flatter me, would see as a charming, lovable light.

Then, on third thoughts, I ask myself the awkward questions. *Why* should I reverberate to this archetype, you to that one? What is the *point* of integrating my personality if the whole thing is going to be snuffed out at death? And what's the *real* link between heaven and earth, planets and personality. When you think about it, it's a chicken-and-egg paradox: which comes first, the heavenly pattern or the human personality? Does the horoscope *force you*, in a cold totalitarian way, to be the person you are? Or does your personality, already in existence before your birth, simply choose the right heavenly moment to make your entrance on Earth's stage?

I cannot say that I've reached clear-cut, dogmatic conclusions yet to these questions. But over the years, veering from one attitude to the other and back again, I've learnt to appreciate all standpoints in the reincarnation issue. I can understand the frustration of scientists coming face to face with irrational beliefs; and I can share the ecstasy of those believers who make genuine, true discoveries about their soul's journey through time. But always, whether I accept reincarnation as a literal or metaphorical truth, I appreciate it best when it is linked to astrology.

About this Book

This book is designed to help you understand your own nature in its totality – where you've been, where you're going, and what is the point of your journey. Since you are one individual among many thousands of readers, it is written for you – but not for you alone. So it is full of general remarks and sweeping statements that can apply, in one way or other, to a large number of people. Try not to be turned off by this. When you read the sections that apply to you, accept that they are written for many eyes – but accept, too, that they are the result of much careful meditation on my part. If you read carefully, your own intuition will be triggered into action and you will see clearly – clairvoyantly – the truth within your soul.

I am not trying to convert you to a definite belief in reincarnation. I do suggest, however, that it's a worthwhile metaphysical game to play – and like all good sports-people you should take the game seriously while playing. In the end, you may decide that this particular imaginative model of the universe does not really suit you. Equally though, you may find that it changes your whole outlook on life.

Whatever your final view, I hope that reading this book will make you think about yourself – and your friends – in a new and interesting way.

But remember – these aren't really new ideas at all. If you recognize the truth in this book, you are really remembering something that you knew a long time ago, in another life. Now, in this life, you have the chance to develop this knowledge.

I'll give you an example. Three and a half centuries ago, speaking to his friend William Drummond, old Ben Jonson admitted that he 'cast horoscopes, but do not trust them'.

Perhaps this book will help to change his mind.

CHAPTER TWO

Dramarathon

You won't find the word *dramarathon* in the dictionary, for the good reason that I've just made it up. As you can see, it's a simple amalgam of *drama* and *marathon,* and is meant to convey the idea of reincarnation as a kind of long-running theatre show.

You join this theatre company in the same way that William Shakespeare joined the Burbage players: as a nobody, holding horses outside the stage entrance. But gradually, with experience, you become a spear-carrying extra, then a walk-on with a few lines to say, then perhaps a clown for the Christmas panto, understudy for one of the leading actors, ingénue in a farce until, after a number of years, you attain the giddy heights of a leading player, with your name on top of the play-bill and the audience in raptures at curtain-fall.

This is what happens to all of us, if the reincarnation myth is true. All the world's a stage, and everyone alive is an actor in its never-ending pageant. Even when you die, you don't actually *die*, but gracefully retire to your dressing-room, resting awhile before donning a new costume and new make-up and striding on-stage for a new role in the non-stop Dramarathon of life.

There are two main developments taking place during this long-running saga. You, as an individual actor, are clearly becoming more skilful with experience. Not only can you essay the more difficult roles in the repertoire, but your range becomes wider; you can dart from musical to tragedy to situation comedy without loss of concentration. In short, you make progress – slowly, stumblingly at first, but learning from your mistakes.

You learn from other members of the company, too. In any collection of humanity there are people with whom you have an instant rapport, and others whom you cannot abide. But in the intense, hot-house atmosphere of a theatre company you are thrown together, whether you like each other or not. You simulate emotions of tenderness and love towards someone whom, in reality, you positively dislike; and gradually, by being forced to work together, you adapt to him, and he to you, until you learn to understand and, who knows, love one another.

In real life, too, people are thrown together in groups that are not of their own choosing. In families, schools or workplaces, you are forced to mix with people who are different from yourselves; but by mixing, you widen your experience of human life and develop your own potential. These meetings – between mother and child, child and teacher, apprentice and foreman – seem totally fortuitous; but in the Dramarathon there are no accidental relationships. The people you meet are those whom you have met – and loved and quarrelled with – many times before, in many earlier incarnations. Clearly you do make *some* new friends and enemies in a lifetime; but once the contact is made, the relationships will continue at another time, another place, in different personalities.

In the repertory theatre you may play the hero one week, the villain the next. You could switch from Hamlet, full of self-doubts and introspection, to Henry V, burning with confidence and ardour, and back to the man of conscience, Brutus, and forward to the lovable old rogue, Falstaff. You could even play Rosalind in *As You Like It*, for on the stage actors and actresses swop sex in the twinkling of a costume.

In just the same way, in the Dramarathon you swop roles and sexes in the twinkling of a lifetime. In your current life you may be an ebullient party-goer; but back in the 18th century you could have been a shy little cabinet-maker devoted

to your craft, and by the 22nd century you could be the leader
of a space-colonising mission.

But that makes the process sound altogether too accidental.
In fact, there's a very shrewd casting-director at work, always
picking exactly the right role for you to play in any particular
life. For even when you become a star, you do not always play
the leading part; sometimes you might take a cameo role, a
small part that still calls for a great deal of subtle dramatic
technique. Equally, you may be quite a beginner but still be
allowed a stab at an important, demanding role.

Exactly who the casting-director may be is a moot point. It
might be God or one of his Executive Archangels in charge of
Forward Planning; or it might be yourself, talking things over
with the archangel before rehearsals begin; or it might be
nobody: just a cold, anonymous Fate pinning up the cast-list
on the notice board, with no questions asked and no
explanations given.

In outline, that's the first path of development that takes
place in the Dramarathon. But there's also another, larger
dimension: the progress made by the whole theatre company,
the whole human race.

It's frequently said by cynics that mankind never makes any
progress. Look at history, they exclaim, and look at current
affairs – today we are committing the same follies and
barbarities that were practised in any of the so-called primitive
cultures. If anything, they say, we are *worse*, for the cruelties of
this century are on a far larger scale than was ever possible
before. No prehistoric African tribal dictator could commit the
wholesale genocide of Ugandans that Amin, with his trained
secret police, could accomplish; and Attila the Hun didn't
have the firepower and modern organization to rival the
achievements of the Third Reich.

But this begs the question: What is progress? One hundred
years ago, a Westerner would see progress in terms of colonial
expansion. Ten years ago, he would have seen it in terms of

scientific development. Today we are not sure; or perhaps we are readier to admit that there are many kinds of progress, each one as valid as the rest.

Certainly our own worldly consciousness may not be the best judge of true spiritual progress, just as the standards of the coach trade ('I like a good laugh when I go out for some entertainment') are not necessarily the same as those of the artistic director of the theatre company. He sets his sights on something altogether more sublime: true artistry, dramatic integrity, the highest expression of theatrical culture. And over a long period he can see the improvements in individual performers as well as the company as a whole – which has, in his time, changed from a third-rate amateur dramatic society to something much more professional.

He's a shrewd fellow, this Good Old Director (known as God, for short). He isn't fooled by the big hammy performance or the clever little vignette full of fake mannerisms. He looks for clear, bell-like honesty, which he can find as easily in a one-line walk-on part as he can in the centre-stage primadonna performances. He's impressed by teamwork – by the willingness of a player to co-operate with other actors, not to hog the limelight or cap other people's stories or bristle with self-importance. Above all, he looks for soulfulness: the ability of great actors to embody the frailty and joy and numinosity of the human condition in whatever role they play.

So progress is made in the Dramarathon. The same old plays are rehearsed season after season. The same old stories are dramatized over and over again, and each time the performances are as fresh as a daisy, as though the actors had never played these parts before. But if you compared the performances nowadays with those of a few millennia ago, you would soon see the difference. There's a greater rounding-out of character; and whereas, in the old days, there would be only a handful of actors capable of playing well, today the talent is much more widely spread.

Obviously the real process of life, death and rebirth isn't actually a theatrical performance, so the simile shouldn't be taken literally. But the Dramarathon is still a useful and viable concept which I shall employ throughout this book: the concept of eternal life shared between Earth and heaven, with each visit to Earth made in a different personality.

Who Believes in Reincarnation?

The idea of rebirth is as old as the hills. Two thousand years ago, to judge by anthropological studies, the majority of people living in the world believed in some kind of personal renewal or resurrection or transmigration from one body to another. The concept was widely held throughout the American Indian tribes, the Mayans of Central America, the Icannas of the Amazonian rain-forests. Many tropical African peoples, from the Zulus in the south to the Ibo in the west, had deep-seated beliefs in reincarnation. It was a belief shared by most early European cultures, from Iceland to old Prussia, including the Celts of ancient Britain. In Australia, every aboriginal tribe without exception believed in the return of ancestors as new babies. Most of all, the peoples of the Indian sub-continent – the Dravidians and Nagas in particular – and South-East Asia as far as the Malay peninsula, all had an abiding faith in rebirth.

For it was here that the two great religions of Hinduism and Buddhism were born, both of which have reincarnation as a central tenet. And it was in India that the idea of the spiritual Dramarathon was developed until it became part of everyday Hindu and Buddhist consciousness. It's nicely put in *Echoes from the Orient*:

> In the East the life of man is held to be a pilgrimage, not only from the cradle to the grave, but also through that vast period of time, stretching from the beginning to the end of a

Manvantara, or period of evolution... Nations and civilizations rise, grow old, decline and disappear; but man lives on, spectator of all the innumerable changes of environment... He gathers experience in all ages, under all rulers, civilizations and customs, ever engaged in a pilgrimage to the shrine from whence he came.

The same idea is expressed, more poetically, in the *Bhagavad-Gita*:

> There is day and night in the universe.
> Day dawns, and all those lives that lay hidden asleep
> Come forth and show themselves, mortally manifest;
> Night falls, and all are dissolved
> Into the sleeping germ of life.
> Thus they are seen, O Prince, and appear unceasingly,
> Dissolving with the dark, and with day returning
> Back to the new birth, new death...

It's easy to see how unsophisticated rural people, constantly aware of the cyclic flow of the seasons, might compare human life with flowers, crops and plants, which seem to die in the autumn, only to be reborn the following spring. If that were all there is to reincarnation, it would be simply a sentimentality – a reassurance, directed at simple folk, that dying was not *adieu* but *au revoir*.

But it is linked, notably in Buddhism, with a complex idea of evolution that explains where man came from – and where he's going. As Edwin Burt wrote in *Teachings of the compassionate Buddha*:

> First and quite central is the concept of Brahman, the metaphysical absolute. Out of Brahman come all things; to Brahman all things return. Second, there is the concept of *atman*, the soul or self. And the very meaning of this concept is determined by the central Hindu conviction that the true self of each human being is identical with

Brahman, and that when that identity is realized the quest for salvation is realized.

So far these ideas are not dissimilar from those of Christianity or many other religions: that man has a spark of God within him, and that when all ungodliness has been washed away, man will be reunited with his creator.

In Christianity, of course, this purification must take place within a single lifetime, whether it lasts a month or a century. According to how well you've scrubbed your soul on Earth, you are rewarded with an eternal holiday in Heaven, or eternal damnation elsewhere.

Hinduism and Buddhism, on the other hand, adopt a more reasonable and logical approach. The aim remains the same: the washing away of worldly cravings. But the time-scale is appropriately lengthened:

> Only in rare cases will an individual be sufficiently purged of these cravings in his present existence so that he can hope for liberation before the death of the body his soul now tenants. But this soul will survive this event and continue to exist, taking new forms one after another until the purgation is complete; in fact, it has existed in innumerable forms in the past.

Thus the Christian is admonished to behave well in one lifetime, for the sake of eternal happiness or misery in the hereafter – as though he were a gambler urged by his bookmaker to place all his wealth on an outsider. If the horse wins, well and good – if not, everything is lost.

The follower of Buddha, on the other hand, is given all the time in the world to attain *nirvana*, much as a do-it-yourself handyman can take his time renovating his own house. If he does a poor job, he will have to tackle the job again...and again...until he learns to be an expert; and in the meantime, he's the one who suffers, living in a half-completed home.

This belief that a man is responsible for his own actions is echoed in the Christian religion, of course; and it's widely understood that some early Church Fathers, notably Origen (185–254 AD), believed not only in rebirth but also in karma:

> Everyone, therefore, of those who descend to the earth is, according to his deserts or to his position that he had there, ordained to be born in this world either in a different place, or in a different nation, or in a different occupation, or with different infirmities, or to be descended from religious or at least less pious parents; so as sometimes to bring about that an Israelite descends among the Scythians, and a poor Egyptian is brought down to Judaea.

Many New Testament sayings can be used to support the notion that Jesus himself accepted reincarnation and karma as religious truisms of his age. Whatever a man sows, he shall also reap. Judge not, that you be not judged. Certainly the influence of Greek thinkers would have spread the ideas among Mediterranean intellectuals. Plato is perhaps the most celebrated believer in rebirth and the law of cause and effect. As he wrote in his *Laws*:

> Know that if you become worse you will go to the worse souls, or if better to the better, and in every succession of life and death you will do and suffer what like may fitly suffer at the hands of like.

But as orthodox Christianity gained a stranglehold on Western thought, reincarnation was no longer spoken about; and in 555 AD, at the Fifth Ecumenical Council, the teachings of 'the pre-existence of the soul' were pronounced anathema.

It became, literally, an occult topic, hidden from public consideration. And although many individual philosophers have believed in rebirth, it has never been generally accepted in the West.

With the rise of several non-conformist cults during the late 19th century – notably theosophy and anthroposophy – a merging took place between Eastern and Christian attitudes. Most of the spiritual groups and churches that profess a belief in reincarnation today can trace their intellectual ancestry back to the theosophical movement.

The 20th century has introduced one new voice into the argument: that of the psychologist Carl Jung, who did more than anyone to marry religious and psychological views together. In a lecture given in 1939, he said:

> Rebirth is not a process that we can in any way observe. We can neither measure nor weigh nor photograph it. It is entirely beyond sense perceptions. We have to deal here with a purely psychic reality, which is transmitted to us only indirectly. One speaks of rebirth; one professes rebirth; one is filled with rebirth.
>
> Rebirth is an affirmation that must be counted among the primordial affirmations of mankind. These affirmations must be based on what I call archetypes.

To Jung, it didn't matter whether reincarnation was a fact. What was significant was that many people, in many different cultures, believed it to be true. Easter is one collective affirmation of the Rebirth archetype; so indeed, is Christmas, for in the northern hemisphere it's at Christmas that the days start to lengthen again; and the Romans called this festival The Birth of the Unconquered Sun.

Just as whole communities celebrate the Rebirth archetype, so do individuals. Anyone who turns over a new leaf, wipes the slate clean, forgives and forgets is embodying the Rebirth archetype; and so, of course, are all the born-again Christians. To Jung and his followers, Rebirth is a psychic reality: a kind of giant shadowy whale swimming in the waters of the Collective Unconscious, a creature you can hardly avoid once you delve beneath material waters into these submarine depths.

I leave you to decide what your attitude to Rebirth shall be.

Believe it totally, by all means. Eventually, if you wish, snuckle it to ridicule. But while you read this book, play the metaphysical game of *assuming* the idea of reincarnation to be true. There are arguments for and against; but don't be completely swayed either way. To appreciate the Dramarathon you must, as Aristotle said, suspend your disbelief.

Arguments For and Against

There are five points commonly raised in the defence – or demolition – of astrology. You can take one side or the other – or come up on the fence beside me!

1. I've been here before. Many of us have experienced what's called *déjà vu* – the feeling that we've been to this mansion or landscape or country before; that we recognize that stranger across the street; that a distant memory is triggered when we sit at this antique table, drink from this 18th-century glass, handle this little Etruscan figurine.

It can easily be explained, says the pro-reincarnation lobby, by the probability that we have lived many times before – in that house, that country; knowing that stranger, owning that table, that glassware; and ourselves modelling that little figurine.

Rubbish, says the anti-brigade. The true explanation, they assert, is that the house, stranger or table is *similar* in some respects to a house, person or table we know already, but cannot quite recall for the moment. Alternatively, they suggest, our brain-circuits occasionally, like stunt aircraft, do a loop-the-loop, registering a vision and then, a millisecond later, registering once again. What we are recognizing is not a memory from two hundred years ago – merely a millisecond ago.

2. I Was There. Occasionally, many of us have a dream or waking vision that we were at the Battle of Agincourt, or helping to dress Mary Queen of Scot's hair, or smoking the pipe of peace outside the Chief's wigwam. These could be interpreted as memories of past lives. Particularly vivid are experiences of death, perhaps involving torture. Is it not likely, runs the argument, that such searing experiences have been traumatized so deeply into the soul that we can have an action replay every once in a while – sometimes in terrifying slow motion.

Big deal, says the anti-brigade. And isn't it interesting that these memories either have a warm, nostalgic, *comforting* glow to them, or they are the stuff of nightmares and horror movies? Isn't it fascinating that they usually involve a famous historical figure (about whom you've read a great deal) or an equally celebrated form of death (burning at the stake is Top of the Toppings, closely followed by crucifixion)?

3. I Was Mary Queen of Scots. Occasionally some of us have a clear indication that we were a particular person in the past. This may be merely a glimpse, or a recurring vision. It may be an experience totally private and personal; or one suggested by another person, such as a medium or guru; or one that's been brought up from the Unconscious through hypnotic regression or meditation.

This kind of evidence is growing, and growing more convincing with every new piece of research on the subject. For personal memories, the *doyenne* is Joan Grant, who has written many books recalling lives in Egypt, Greece and elsewhere. For former lives described by a medium, the most fluent exponent was Edgar Cayce, whose remarkable testimony in many thousands of cases has been faithfully recorded by his disciples. And for lives recalled through hypnosis, the evidence is mounting every year – from the original *Search for Bridey Murphy* through to Helen

Wambach's *Life Before Life*. To find details of these and other testimonies, consult Chapter Twelve, LEARNING MORE.

This 'proof', more than any other, is the one that the anti-reincarnation boys really enjoy bashing to smithereens. They sneer at anyone who thinks he was any kind of celebrity in the past; and they condemn the whole exercise as a mild form of obsessive schizophrenia – the sort of thing which, taken to extremes, lands people in the looney-bin thinking they're Napoleon.

Their explanation for regressive phenomena is twofold. Some of them assert that there's a genetic memory-bank capable of being inherited by successive generations. Somewhere in your brain, they suggest, there's a cupboard full of 17th-, 18th- and 19th-century recollections – memories that have been genetically passed from parent to child to grandchild.

Their second explanation, which Jungians might accept, is that under hypnotic regression you are simply diving into the waters of the Collective Unconscious where the debris of all human life since the year dot lies scattered on the ocean floor, like so much shipwrecked treasure. Because all skin-divers, given half a chance, believe in Finders Keepers, you automatically like to think that the flotsam you discover belongs to you, whereas in reality it belongs to everybody.

If I may add a word from my vantage-point on the fence, I know at least three ladies who believe they were Mary Queen of Scots. They could be deluded; but a plausible explanation is that they were all ardent Roman Catholics in 16th-century Europe. Since Mary was the great rallying figure for the Counter-Reformation in northern Europe, she was the object of many hopes and prayers – and much adoration. The image of Mary was burned into the soul of these people – so much so that they still identify with her – literally – four centuries later.

4. Childhood prodigies. There are exceptional people who seem able to play the piano in the high chair, tackle quadratic equations in the cot, and start writing poetry in the pram. It's almost as though they were Mozart, Einstein or Ben Jonson back in mortal life again.

Oh yeah, sneer the antis. If there were such a thing as a prodigy, it would be an accident of nature, a freak of the chromosomes. But on the whole, they say, talent is nurtured, not inborn, a matter of environment, not innate characteristics.

This is a pretty rotten argument, if you ask me. Increasingly it's being shown that people have personalities from the moment of birth. The nine months in the womb is not spent simply forming the body; it forms the mind and emotional outlook as well.

We just *said* that, reply the biologists in their condescending way. We just explained, if you'd only listen, that innate characteristics are due to body chemistry, nothing else.

How do you know, buster? I reply, jumping down off the fence. How do you *know* that nothing else is involved? Has it occurred to you that the genetic code might actually be commands from a higher level of life? You resemble the builder who thinks that plans appear at random through the mail; he refuses to believe that an architect actually posted them.

Ha ha, say the biologists sardonically. We haven't found *any* proof anywhere that the architect exists.

Then find some, I snarl, clambering back.

To take part in these metaphysical debates, you've got to be damn fit.

5. Commonsense. Once you start thinking about the purpose of life, the Dramarathon makes good sense. It provides a *reason* for living, and ensures *justice* for all. The purpose of life is to make you a perfect all-rounder, brilliant at everything, like a magnificently polished diamond; and to accomplish this, you work at one facet at a time. Whatever you do and say and think in this life will have its inevitable consequence in lives to come. You cannot escape your destiny, for you have created it yourself. Act like a bastard now, and you'll pay for your cruelty later. Be good, and you'll be rewarded.

The objection to this little homily is a good-natured yawn. Believe whatever makes you happy, says the anti-brigade – but don't expect us to go along with your sentimental, goody-two-shoes twaddle.

More seriously, don't you realize that we know a good deal about evolution nowadays? All the fairy-tale beliefs of the past, like a golden age or Atlantis or visits from spacemen, have been shown to be balderdash. Our past is neither romantic nor moral nor commonsensical. We simply happened. We are clever animals, with a huge, newly developed brain that is, as far as we know, the only *self-conscious* brain in nature. As part of this self-consciousness, we have developed a liking – almost an addiction – for inventing fantasies about our past and our future. They are only fantasies. There is no heaven, no hell, no hereafter, no pre-existence or post-existence. Oh, and one final point: this garbage about astrology. Throw it away: it's starting to stink. Grow up. Be an atheist like us.

With one bound I leap from the fence. It's time I taught these snucklers a lesson.

CHAPTER THREE

Scenarios in the Sky

To the scientific observer, armed with telescopes and space probes and wall-to-wall computers, the sky has become known territory. Once, in medieval times, it was considered a blue crystal sphere suspended above Earth; and the stars were countless tiny windows open to the brilliant light of Heaven beyond. Poetic, say the scientists, but untrue.

Nowadays we know much more. The sky is a universe, unimaginably vast and getting vaster by the minute, filled with particles, gas clouds, rocks and flames and suns being born and burning bright and dying in magnificent explosions. Put simply, it is a factory for making atoms, and much of it is catalogued, measured and, so the scientists think, understood fairly well.

But not well enough, for this new explanation of the sky, while solving some mysteries, creates many more. To begin at the beginning. Scientists scoff at the creation story in Genesis, maintaining that there was no God, no void, no darkness upon the face of the deep; and, truth to tell, it is a pretty incredible story. But the scientists' version, developed in the last few years, is equally daft. They assert that the universe began 20 billion years ago with a Big Bang. Before the Bang there was nothing: no space, no time, nothing at all. Then, out of nowhere, the universe exploded – the biggest explosion ever, so big that it burst the whole universe, every ton of it, outwards with a force that is still at work. We are still expanding. Each galaxy is still racing away from the rest, at a current speed of 40 miles a second, and the scientists have no idea whether it will ever end.

It may, for all they know, expand for ever: a one-way ticket to infinity, with all the stars gradually disappearing from each other's sight. Or, as an alternative theory, it may stop, pause, and start imploding, gradually picking up speed as it zooms in again towards – once more – what's called a singularity, a nothingness.

There are variations on this theme. Some scientists believe that the universe never quite reaches this singularity. Instead, it bounces out again, and back again, in and out like a vast lung breathing every 100 billion years. Other scientists even suggest our whole universe, once it returns to singularity, becomes one particle in an immeasurably larger universe elsewhere.

No doubt there will be plenty of new hypotheses in the years ahead. The point to note is that scientists are quite prepared to put forward the most far-fetched ideas to explain the inexplicable. They will even step outside their own laws of physics and chemistry, abandoning the sacred principle of cause and effect, to show how a universe comes into existence.

Now let's consider life on earth. Biologists, like astronomers, know a great deal now about the *mechanisms* of their subject, and can deftly show how life replicates and diversifies and survives in this world of ours. But all their laws of biochemistry must be abandoned when they try to explain the *origin* of life on this planet. They fall back on the concept of 'spontaneous generation': that, by chance, over a long period of time, the right proportion of inorganic gases were irradiated by ultraviolet sunlight to form prebiotic molecules – the start of life.

The astronomer Fred Hoyle, in *Life Cloud*, has ridiculed this idea as absurdly unlikely – but has put forward an equally bizarre possibility: that four billion years ago, a comet crashed on Earth bringing with it the first living organisms. In a sense, we came from outer space.

So don't be fooled by the cosy day-to-day reality of life on earth. We are not living in a self-contained little world. Instead, we are children of the universe. Our first spark of life could have flown here from a distant galaxy, and, besides, every atom of our bodies was created billions of years ago, far out in space. Equally, the universe we inhabit is, according to the scientists, utterly mysterious. To explain it, they invent different worlds, different timescales.

Perhaps, after all, there is a truth – a *metaphorical* truth – in the old medieval ideas. There may not be a literal heaven out there in space; but surely, out there among the twinkling stars, there could be something – some device or mechanism or other – to explain how and why we ever got into this space-time continuum in the first place.

That device, as far as I'm concerned, is astrology.

How the Play Was Written

Astrologers believe that the positions of the Sun, Moon and planets at the time of birth have some connection with the kind of person you become. Exactly how this connection works – whether it's a direct influence, or a symptom of something else – is still unknown. To my mind, the most likely explanation is that the horoscope resembles the indicator-board at an airport, telling us which planes will arrive and depart but not actually controlling the aircraft itself. According to this analogy, the horoscope tells the story of your personality. Within limits, it gives the scenario of your life, the script that you are performing at this stage of your Dramarathon. But who wrote the play, and why, remains a mystery.

Well, that isn't quite true. To the ancient astrologers, the Sun, Moon and planets were the source of endless speculation. The Sun, for obvious reasons, was seen as the fount of all power, and was considered to represent and embody the *male* principle in all life. The Moon, meanwhile, due to its changing shape during its monthly cycle, was linked to the *feminine* principle in nature; and these two, male and female intertwining, were the eternal procreative forces ensuring the eternal rhythms of the day and night, spring and autumn, sowing and reaping, birth and death.

The remaining bodies of the Solar System – the planets – were assigned subordinate, but still vital, roles in this grand design. Mars was the aggressive force that produced wars, ill-health and marital strife. Venus, on the other hand, represented all that was fair, lovely and complying. Another pair of planets, Jupiter and Saturn, were also reciprocal in their influence: Jupiter the bringer of prosperity, Saturn the harbinger of bad tidings and despondency. The odd one out, Mercury – possibly because it was so close to the Sun, and always popping in and out of vision – was considered the messenger of the other planets, the errand boy carrying missives between heaven and Earth.

Or between Gods and mortals, of course – for everybody in the ancient world thought of the Sun as Apollo (in Greece), Atum (in Egypt), El Belus (in Babylon), Sol (in Rome), Indra (in India), Mithras (in Persia) or Quetzalcoatl (in Central America). The Moon and planets were also deities in their own right. From their home in the sky, they ruled the Earth – sometimes according to preordained destiny, sometimes through mere temporary caprice. The purpose of human life was simply to obey the gods' instructions, worship them, and keep out of trouble.

To the peoples of the ancient world, therefore, the scenario of their lives was written by gods. They, the human puppets, could not deviate from this script, though, by ingratiating themselves into the gods' good graces, they could try to lessen the bad tidings.

Today there are still a few astrologers who believe in the planets as gods. Most of us, however, have rejected the concept of gods and goddesses ruling Earth from heaven. But what's extraordinary is that, even though ancient astrologers had – to our way of thinking – a quaint cosmology, it still yielded accurate results. The qualities ascribed to the planets 2000 years ago are still valid today. It can be demonstrated, by strict statistical methods, that Mars in the horoscope *does* correlate with anger, competitiveness and a blunt approach to life. Saturn *does* correspond to a serious, materialistic view of life. Jupiter *does* have a link with optimism and self-confidence.

If not gods, then what? Most modern astrologers would say that the Sun, Moon and planets correspond to *life-principles* such as the Jungian archetypes. All life, they would maintain, must be composed of these ingredients, but in different proportions. You, let's say, have Saturn more strongly than I, whereas I have Jupiter and Mars more strongly than you.

Modern astrologers would also differ from their ancient counterparts in the matter of predestination and freewill. They would assert that the horoscope indicates only the trends in your life, not the certainties. To go back to the metaphor mentioned in Chapter One, the weather forecast does not order you to go on a picnic, or force you to stay at home. The choice is yours; but it's a choice that's made in the light of the prevailing conditions. In just the same way, astrologers nowadays would say that you can try to lead whatever lifestyle you want; but in the end you are guided, nudged and drawn along the paths indicated by your horoscope.

In other words, you are given a character in a particular play, but you are free to improvise within limits.

I go along with this astrological view of life, with one proviso: it's based on a planetary pattern that was established a long time ago – in fact, about 4.5 billion years ago, soon after the formation of the Solar System. Obviously there are minor adjustments to the planetary orbits taking place all the time, for a variety of reasons: slowing down, gravitational pulls and, who knows, the occasional stunning entry of a large visiting comet from outer space. But, on the whole, Saturn is exactly *there*, in that particular part of the sky, because that's the way the Solar System was formed, 4.5 billion years ago.

The implication is clear. Your personality in this life was somehow thought of, or taken into consideration, or planned for, all those mind-boggling aeons ago. You are not an accident. You are a child of the Solar System, built into the fabric of the universe.

Why the Play Was Written

It's a great puzzle, even to those who believe in astrology, why these huge lumps of rock and gas out in space should have anything to do with human life on Earth. Probably we shall have to make many new astrophysical and biological discoveries before we can understand how the system works. But there are certain obvious avenues of enquiry.

In the first place, we've already seen how orthodox scientists find it impossible to explain the creation of the universe in terms of ordinary physical laws. It's as though our space-time continuum is a self-contained, closed system, like a tin of beans. Actually, that's not a very good analogy, because the tin of beans exists within a larger space-time continuum, which we comprehend even if the beans do not. A better possible metaphor would be the ordinary family drawing-room, with Dad watching TV, Mum knitting, and the kids doing homework. They all exist in the same space, but they inhabit different universes. Dad is totally encased in a world called *Sportsnight*, Mum in her own musings, the kids in the teacher's questions. At any time, of course, the spell can be broken, and they merge back into a common world of chit-chat and coffee-making. But each lives in his own consciousness. Each creates his own world through his own imagination – Dad least of all, because it's created for him by television, Mum a bit more so (though look, she's falling asleep, she's moving into a deeper, more mysterious universe yet), and the children a great deal, for their minds are constructing ideas, arguments, pictures as they complete their homework.

I've said that the spell can be broken, and the worlds merge together. But there's another kind of interaction taking place, too. One of the children, writing a poem, is influenced not only by the sound of the commentary but by the excitement within Dad's mind as the match reaches its climax. And her poem, created within her own imagination, is somehow part of Mum's dream, too. In a modest, homely way, unconscious telepathy is taking place.

This is so common, if unprovable, that you are bound to recognize the phenomenon. Worlds within worlds. Instant rapport between apparently separate universes. Something like this must take place in the physical universe. There must be means of communication between one space-time continuum and another. If you believe in the Dramarathon, there must be a dressing-room somewhere that you retire to between one life and the next. It could be elsewhere in our galaxy, I suppose. It could, when you think about it, be *here*, occupying the same space but not the same time – the past and the future co-existing with the present, but at different frequencies. It *could* be that this whole universe, so real and measurable and self-contained, is actually a world of imagination, a tremendously vivid dream of everyone who lives within it.

Whatever fanciful hypothesis we prefer, we still need to find a means of communication – a doorway between heaven and Earth. Which brings us neatly back to the medieval notion of the stars being windows through which the heavenly brilliance beyond can be glimpsed.

Perhaps the Solar System is our electrical transformer, changing the heavenly voltage down to our own potential. Perhaps it's a kind of combination lock, its pattern endlessly changing, so that only a particular kind of spiritual energy can be passed through the doorway into earthly life. With every minute that passes, each planet has moved further along its appointed orbit, and the Earth has turned further on its axis. With every minute that passes, a *unique* pattern is created. (Not quite: it could be reproduced every seven billion *billion* years – but by that time the universe will have breathed in and out at least 70 million times, and our own little Solar System will have disappeared before the very first breath is over!)

Grammar of the Play

But even though the pattern of the sky is never the same, certain similarities recur. You know, of course, that the path along which the Sun, Moon and planets seem to travel through the sky is known as the Zodiac; and that this Zodiac is divided into twelve equal segments, known as the Zodiac signs. The simplest recurrence is the passage of the Sun through these Zodiac signs once every year. Every January it returns to Capricorn, every February to Pisces, and so on, passing through one sign every month and the whole sky every twelvemonth.

Even quicker is the Moon, which passes through each sign in a mere two and half days. The planets, being further away, take longer. The most distant of all, Pluto, takes 250 years to traverse the whole sky. But it's a regular motion. Pluto today is roughly in the same position that it occupied in 1730; and it'll be there again around 2230 AD.

There are other recognized patterns that planets make to each other. Whenever the Sun and Moon appear in a straight line from Earth, an eclipse – or, as it's also called, a conjunction – takes place. Fourteen days later, at the Full Moon, they're opposite each other, so an opposition takes place. Similar so-called *aspects* take place frequently between different planets; and whenever this happens, there's a special spark struck: a kind of short circuit in this electrical transformer.

In psychological terms, anyone born during a particular aspect will embody the qualities of that aspect. To take a simple example: Richard Widmark, George C. Scott and Edward Kennedy were all born when the Sun was side by side with Mars. All these men self-evidently have a lot of energy, competitiveness and pride in their manhood. However different they are in other ways, this common thread of virile power runs through the three of them – all due to this conjunction between Sun and macho Mars.

It's due to these recurring similarities that I can attempt to trace a pattern between one life and the next. If, as I believe, there are links between your life today and the lives you have already passed on Earth, these should be apparent in your horoscope.

They are shown in the positions of the Sun, Moon and planets, according to their Zodiac signs and aspects, and in relation to two special points in the sky: the East Point and the Moon's Node.

These are the basic elements of astrology – the grammar, if you like, of the scenario written in the sky at your birth. But before you see how all these factors relate to your past lives, you must think more about the Dramarathon itself: its shape, its scenes, its story-line.

CHAPTER FOUR

Plays and Players

To run the Dramarathon you need stamina. In the course of many millennia – at least 300,000 years, by my reckoning, but probably more – you will incarnate as saint and sinner, rich man, poor man, male and female. Your skin will be black, yellow, pink, olive, your nationality anything from Lapp to Turk, Russian to Prussian, Dutch to Polynesian.

You will die in the cradle, in warfare, in comfort and in the geriatric ward. And in between birth and death, you will experience everything – all the pains and joys, triumphs and failures known to humanity. By the end of it all, you'll be a man, my son.

The process, as I say, lasts a long time. Exactly how long is not known. Some people, thinking of the so-called Great Year – the time it takes for the Zodiac to precess all the way round the constellations – say 25,000 years. The Indians, who call this time-cycle the *kalpa*, say much longer – so long that a fixed number of years cannot be attached to it. The Theosophists agree. They regard re-embodiment as the universal condition of spiritual evolution. According to them, you can never outgrow the need for fresh experience and new cycles of incarnations. For them the Dramarathon is endless.

It's also unique to you, to me, to any individual. Although each Dramarathon undoubtedly resembles the others in overall structure and purpose, it's still original – a one-off experience that no other soul has had in quite the same way. Believe it or not, *you* are making a unique contribution to the history of the Universe!

Most religions that have reincarnation as part of their doctrine agree that the process goes something like this. Every

so often, at the start of a new cycle or whenever, God gives
birth to a new batch of souls: very innocent and pure and
inexperienced souls, still living, so to speak, in the Garden of
Eden. But as their lives increase, they gradually become more
worldly, more material, more separated from God, until, at the
nadir of their cycle, they are immersed in earthliness. They
seem quite unGod-like; but within them, so the doctrine runs,
is still the original divine spark that gave them birth in the first
place. Their task, in the second, upward half of the cycle, is to
develop this goodness so that it grows and permeates every
particle of their soul. Then they can be reunited with God,
their original Father and Mother – long-lost babies welcomed
home as mature and capable adults.

What happens then is anyone's guess. You may clear off to
the advanced training college on the Andromeda galaxy and
start the process over again, this time at a higher level. But this
simple idea of spiritual evolution, developed by people
without any knowledge of modern science, does bear an
uncanny resemblance to the process of *material* evolution. Our
Solar System, for instance, was born out of a primordial gas
cloud, with the atoms floating free and 'innocent'. Then,
gradually, through the force of gravity, these atoms are tugged
into material shape, crushed into the lattice shapes of metal
and stone so that they become immovable, imprisoned, locked
away in the dungeons of Earth.

Then a remarkable event happens. The more 'evolved'
atoms co-operate to become molecules which, at a certain
stage, develop the unique capacity to replicate themselves. Life
on Earth is born. Molecules become cells. Cells become
bodies. Bodies become human communities. And, eventually,
these humans develop craft that can take the atoms out into
free space again – this time as developed, organized, 'adult'
bits of matter.

You may find this analogy a shade too fanciful, but it is
interesting how the evolution of matter seems to be on a

similar logarithmic timescale to that of spirit. Both of them, since the Big Bang, are accelerating. The process of evolution is exceedingly slow at the beginning, becoming increasingly rapid as forms get more complex and inter-related until, who knows, we move into a higher octave altogether.

The astronomer Carl Sagan, in *The Dragons of Eden*, has given a fascinating timetable of material development. If you compress the whole history of the universe into a single year, life on Earth takes a mighty long time to evolve. The Big Bang takes place on New Year's Day. By May our galaxy, the Milky Way, is beginning to form. By September the Solar System is created. October sees the development of the very earliest life-forms – algae and bacteria and the like. Not until mid-November do the first plants appear. Worms evolve on December 16th, fish on the 19th, insects on the 21st, reptiles on the 23rd, mammals on Boxing Day, birds the day after, flowers on the 28th, primates on the 29th and, glory be, the first humans on New Year's Eve, around 10.30 in the evening. In fact, everything that we would describe as civilization – from cave-men onwards – has taken place in the final *two minutes of the year!*

So the Dramarathon, in contrast to ordinary road-races, starts off at a crawl and accelerates to a sprint. But whereas the normal long-distance runner would soon collapse from strain, the Dramarathon runner seems able to keep up without any noticeable discomfort. There are two reasons for this: first, he gets plenty of rest in between lives, and secondly, he simply isn't aware that the pace is hotting up. Life in Concorde seems to be just the same, whether you're taxi-ing for take-off or breaking the sound barrier. It's the same on the Dramarathon.

This speeding-up of evolution involves increasingly more frequent lives on Earth. In the wild, nomadic days of pre-history, life barely changed from one millennium to the next. Souls were slowly immersing themselves in earthly life, with long gaps between incarnations to recover from the shock. In addition, because there was so little individuality, a number of newly-formed souls might incarnate in the same body, as a kind of package trip from heaven, all sharing the same food, the same sunshine, the same lifestyle, because they simply weren't ready for a more personalized experience.

Virtually everyone alive today is on the path of individual selfhood. Even the Stone Age natives of New Guinea and Brazil are being hurried into clearcut individuality, with more choices - and problems - open to them than ever before.

There are more people than ever before on Earth today - more than 4000 million of us. Heaven's a pretty empty place these days, for the good reason that every soul wants, if possible, to crowd into Earth during this century. There's a tremendous quickening of consciousness taking place. No one can afford to miss out on the crucial changes happening on Earth at present.

Names of the Game

Before we look at the pattern of individual development from one life to the next, I must define how I'm using certain words from now on.

Your SOUL is the eternal life-form that you're evolving. It's certainly a much bigger and more complex entity than you realize, for in your present lifetime you probably have contact with only a small part of it.

In each lifetime you are born with a particular PERSONALITY that is composed of *some* of your soul-material, much as the actor uses some - but not all - of his own qualities to create a stage character. A few evolved people have close contact between their temporary earthly personality and their eternal soul. They are the saints, the holy men, the natural leaders, the rare people whom we sense to have a rich extra dimension to their lives.

Your personality, although present at birth, can only be developed through life itself. Inevitably it is shaped – and sometimes thwarted – by circumstances. Without these constraints (and chances) from your environment, your personality couldn't live; and so they are the fuel you burn up as you run your Dramarathon. The total experience – personality allied to circumstances – makes up your life. When you die, this experience is distilled and concentrated and packed into the fabric of your eternal soul. Nothing is lost.

Indeed, it's kept for a very good reason. The experiences of your present life will form the structure of your next incarnation, just as the success or failure of one stage-role determines how you will face up to the next part you are offered.

Each personality tends to develop a patina, an outward surface that's obvious to anyone who knows you. This is your EGO. You may be very fond of your ego. It contains all your fads and fancies, self-indulgences and flatteries. When your body dies, it dies too. Only the true inner part of your personality, which I call the SELF, will survive as part of your total soul.

There's another way of looking at both your soul and personality. They are formed of two kinds of spiritual energy which I call SPIRIT and PSYCHE.

Spirit is the male, *yang*-oriented quality in life. It isn't the prerogative of men, of course. Every living form is constructed through an interweaving of spirit and psyche, which, in turn, is the female, *yin*-oriented principle. But men – certainly up until these sexually equal days – tended to develop their spirit, while women tended to develop their psyche. This is a very broad generalization, to which there are many exceptions. In no way is spirit superior to psyche. Each complements the other, and to be a rounded soul you need to have developed both.

Your Key Life

Although you lead your lives in chronological sequence, your spiritual progress is not necessarily quite so linear. Your present life isn't always an exact consequence of the one just before. It may have references to other lives spent a long time ago, or it may even be a completely fresh start, with little relevance to any of your previous lives.

The analogy with the theatre is quite apt. Actors tend to become type-cast if they're not careful, playing the same sort of role over and over again. They prefer to dart here and there among the repertoire, playing comedy one week, tragedy the next – partly because it makes a nice change, but mainly because, by being versatile, they can learn so much more.

It's the same with reincarnation. Sometimes the change is needed simply to widen your experience, and sometimes to concentrate your energies on one facet of life that you might otherwise miss.

This process of cause and effect, called karma, is sometimes portrayed as an agent of retribution, the fell hand of God dropping karate-fashion on the back of your sinful neck. Worse still, it's seen as the action of God the chartered accountant, scrupulously balancing the books of good and evil, with every jot and title recorded in its proper column, before he retires to bed with his goodnight cup of Horlicks.

I prefer to see karma as a creative process, Nature's way of helping all living creatures to become more complex and self-sufficient. Arthur Koestler, in many of his books, has pointed out how the concept of Survival of the Fittest is quite inadequate to explain the diversity and inventive genius of Nature. He has suggested that in material evolution there are certain ground-rules that cannot be broken – but, within these parameters, individual species are free to improvise upon a theme. In *Janus: a summing up* he discusses the classic example of the forelimbs of vertebrates which, whether they serve reptiles, birds, whales or man, show the same basic design of bones, muscles, nerves, etc., and are accordingly called homologous organs. The functions of legs, wings and flippers are quite different, yet they all are variations on a single theme – strategic modifications of a pre-existing structure: the forelimb of the common reptilian ancestor. Once Nature has 'taken out a patent' on a vital organ, she sticks to it, and that organ becomes a stable evolutionary holon. Its basic design seems to be governed by a fixed *evolutionary canon*; while its adaptation to swimming, walking or flying is a matter of evolution's flexible *strategy*.

Spiritual evolution has its own canons, too: the cardinal virtues of love, co-operation, responsibility and so on. To be a mature soul, you need to know how to love your enemies – to recognize a common humanity among your fellow-men. This is the theme; and each of us, in life after life, plays a continuing series of variations on this theme, dancing a jig of three steps forward, two steps back, advancing and retreating until we have learnt, through happy events as well as painful ones, that friendship towards all is a fundamental principle of life that cannot be evaded.

So your Key Life is really the unfinished theme on which you will play some more variations in your current incarnation. It may be one particular life, perhaps the one you have just lived; or it may be an amalgamation of several lives.

Here are some examples. I believe – through astrology and intuition – that former Tory leader EDWARD HEATH's Key Life is a summation of several former incarnations: one as an Egyptian administrator, another as an abbot (or abbess) of a religious order, a third as an 18th-century figure in the East India Company. TONY BENN, on the other hand, has a single former incarnation as his Key Life: that of a 17th-century

Leveller at the time of Cromwell. JIMMY CARTER's Key Life is
a combination of two former existences: one as an autocratic
ruler (in Eastern Europe?) and the other as a beautiful, lazy, extra-
vagant woman who became a religious convert in middle age.

Your present life is designed in response to this Key Life.
The major experiences coming your way are exactly
appropriate to test and develop those facets of your soul that
make up your current personality. By examining yourself
today, you can discern what you were in your last life.

There are four main kinds of life that you could be leading.

A Life of Continuity

Here you are pursuing a similar line of development that you
have followed in earlier incarnations. You are, in effect,
becoming type-cast in the Dramarathon.

When this happens, there are always links between your
horoscope now and the horoscope of your Key Life. You may
be born in the same month, so that the Sun lies in the same
Zodiac sign – but this is not essential. More likely would be
that your Moon-sign in this life is the same as your Sun-sign in
your previous life.

Certainly in the everyday aspects of your life – career,
aptitudes, emotional disposition – there could be many
similarities between Then and Now. You are engaged in a
long-term effort – perhaps to specialize in a particular talent,
perhaps to train a side of your character for a special purpose
in a future life. To take some obvious examples: JOAN OF ARC,
without realizing it at the time, would have spent several lives
training for her special incarnation as the Maid of Orleans.
SIR WINSTON CHURCHILL's life was the culmination of several
incarnations along similar lines. In each case, the resulting
personality was strong, clearcut but somewhat eccentric, like an
inbred pedigree animal. Churchill, in particular, was a mass of

psychological contradictions. In order to do his job in the Second World War, he had been forced to neglect certain aspects of soul-development – notably the softer side of his psyche – that, in consequence, cried out for attention in the midst of his bellicose spirit.

A Life of Reaction

This is a very common lifestyle – indeed, the majority of us are involved in this kind of soul-development.

It means that our present incarnation is a direct reaction to our earlier Key Life. Usually this means that we are paying off bad debts, getting rid of old karma. There are many ways in which this can be done, so this is a list of examples, not a comprehensive catalogue.

1. Physical or mental disability. Many of us suffering from ill-health, whether acute or chronic, are experiencing the consequences of our own behaviour in previous lives.

If you are physically blind, you could have been spiritually blind in an earlier life, turning your gaze away from people who needed your help.

If a vital organ is diseased, you could have damaged another person in that same region ('an eye for an eye') or it could have happened metaphorically. Many people who suffer migraine could have broken someone's heart in a previous life.

If you have a mental illness in this life, you could have been too headstrong and arrogant in your views in an earlier incarnation.

If you are accident-prone through clumsiness, you could have caused danger to others by being too foolhardy in your Key Life.

It's terribly easy to be glib about physical karma, and frankly I doubt whether we should make quick assumptions about why any person is ill. For we must remember that some souls, so the doctrine of karma says, take on the burden of sickness as a charitable gesture to help the whole world, much as monks will pray for everyone, never themselves. This aspect of karma strikes me as a dangerous area in which to be opinionated. Remember the old injunction: judge not, that thou be not judged.

2. Family rows. By this I mean any close relationships to which you are drawn by circumstance or ineluctable fate.

These are a favourite means to force you to confront the consequences of your own actions. If you mistreat your wife in this life, you could be the victim next time round. If you're an emotional vampire in one life, sucking the life-force out of a hapless spouse, the tables will surely be turned at some stage in the future.

More positively, if you start to behave well, you will earn good karma in future lives. A family that radiates happiness has earned the right to their joy through good living in the past.

It's important to note that all adherents to the reincarnation principle believe that you can wash away karma through good thoughts, good actions. The Buddha's Eightfold Path to Serenity was right view, right aim, right speech, right action, right living, right effort, right mindfulness and right contemplation. Get those right, he maintained, and you can't go wrong.

3. Denial. If you misuse a skill or insight in one life, it may be denied to you in the next. If, like me, you long to sing like a lark but are tone-deaf, you may well have misused the art of music in a past life, perhaps as worthless propaganda. (Think how many deaf-and-dumb people will be wandering about in the 22nd century, thanks to the prevalence of advertising in our own century.)

A Dead-End Life

Every so often, through design or mismanagement, a soul needs to experience a dead-end life. It may be the culmination of a series of lives of continuity, or possibly the crescendo of one life of reaction after another, with the lesson never being learnt.

These are the negative paths into the dead-end life. But there are positive routes, too. In order to pass a great moral test, it may be necessary to stack the odds steeply against you. And perhaps to learn the ultimate lesson about a particular aspect of life, you need to be totally committed to it. Only then does triumph or failure have a true significance.

It's easy to see that ADOLF HITLER experienced one kind of dead-end life. At the other extreme, so did JESUS CHRIST.

A Second-Breath Life

Finally, there's a second-breath life, which occurs as a complete break from an earlier stage of development. It can come after any of the other kinds of life, but particularly, of course, after a dead-end experience.

It represents, for some, a holiday – a happy deliverance after a series of hard endeavours. Or it can simply be the start of a long series of new lives of continuity. Either way, it's fun at the time!

CHAPTER FIVE

Reading Your Part

Now that we've considered the theory behind reincarnation you can start deciding what your own spiritual history may have been. You can do so by a combination of astrology, intuition, help from friends and family, and a cool consideration of your own psychology.

Getting in the Right Frame of Mind

Sadly, an author has no control over his readership. However strongly I recommend you to enter a quiet, meditative attitude if you want to understand your own Dramarathon, there will doubtless be some of you who are reading WHO WERE YOU? in the rush hour, or giggling over it with friends, or scanning a page or two in between feeding the baby, listening to the radio and talking to the dog.

If you have any training in meditation, you will know what the appropriate state of mind should be: calm and loving, putting earthly worries aside so that your consciousness is clear, alert and empty, like a deserted beach on a mildly sunny day.

It helps if you can breathe rather more slowly and deeply than usual, in through the nose and out through the mouth. No doubt you'll feel self-conscious at first, but all you need are a few minutes of silence, peace and affection around you. I'm not suggesting that you enter a deep meditation, nor that you need a particularly religious atmosphere; but trying to contact your self, leaving your ego behind, is not as easy as you would think in today's busy-busy world.

Thinking About Yourself

Your next task is to spend some time considering your own nature. Most of us build up a self-image in the course of our lives that bears little resemblance to the person we really are. This image may be a projection of our own desires, or it may be the adaptation we make to suit the desires of others. Here are some examples: the eternal joker (what's he hiding behind that camaraderie?); the housewife and mother (existing only for husband and children, never for herself); the official spokesman (has he a mind of his own?) and the armchair critic (smug in his presumptions).

Once you have worked out the positions of your Sun and Moon (in the next chapter) you can consult Chapters Seven and Eight to gain some insight into your astrological character. But before doing so, do some analysing on your own. Think, first of all, about your SPIRIT. What is the strongest force that motivates you in life? Where are your biggest moral difficulties? Where are your weaknesses, when it comes to handling your own problems and, more crucially still, in dealing with other people? What kind of creature are you?

Then think about your inner PSYCHE. What is your everyday emotional disposition – warm, anxious, friendly, critical or what? How quickly do you respond to events around you – are you organized, fluttery, conservative or looking for the experimental solution all the time? What kind of emotional life do you need – cuddly, possessive, independent, undemanding or what?

Imagine yourself in a crowd. Be an overhead camera zooming downwards to focus for a few seconds on yourself. Try to capture the *essence* of your personality in those fleeting seconds. Try to describe yourself in one sentence.

These are only games, not to be taken too seriously. It might help to get a friend or relative to play the game with you, trying to analyse each other's characters in the same brief, nutshell manner. Then read what I say about you in Chapters Seven and Eight.

Memories of the Past

Now you must consider all those puzzles, insights, dreams, coincidences and psychological obsessions that might have a bearing on your Dramarathon. Here are some of the factors that you must bear in mind.

1. Historical periods. When watching a film, reading a novel, learning history at school or visiting a stately home, is there a particular period in history that specially appeals to you? If so, try to find sensible reasons for this. Is it a particularly romantic period – or made romantic by the writer concerned (Du Maurier, for instance, the Brontës)? Is your experience too limited – in other words, if you've only read the Poldark novels, the most likely historical period to attract you will be 18th-century Cornwall? Are you being over-influenced by other people – your family, for instance, or a friend with an obsessive interest in China or Timbuctoo?

Try to discern the difference between true insight and mere fancy. Dismiss, as much as possible, all those 'wouldn't it be nice if...?' daydreams, separating them from those compulsive inner feelings that yes, I was in the American Civil War or wherever.

2. Foreign countries. The same approach must be applied to any countries or nations to which you feel irrationally attached. Suppose you have a powerful liking for France. This is *not* a memory of a past French incarnation if it is simply based on a liking for garlic or Sacha Distel or the Côte d'Azur. But if you are fascinated by the sound of the language (specially if you've never learnt to speak the lingo), or if you feel an enormous tug towards an unfashionable region that is never mentioned by the French Tourist Board, or, above all, if your love of France is combined with a particular historical period, then you may well be receiving an echo from a former existence.

3. Possessions. You may have a special fondness for an antique, portrait or other possession that you either own or have seen elsewhere. You may be particularly drawn to another family – perhaps a famous Scottish clan or simply a surname which keeps running through your head, even though you may never have met anyone called by the name.

Such longings could be caused by a distant memory of once owning the antique or belonging to that family – or perhaps working for it.

4. Vivid memories. Sometimes a dream or nightmare will keep recurring: perhaps a fearful death, or a confrontation that you would prefer to avoid, or a clearcut picture of a landscape, a face, a word of command, a set of clothes – anything that might, just might, be a memory from a past life.

5. Links with Others. The friends (and enemies) surrounding you in this life will probably have been your companions in earlier lives, too. Be guided by any insights and memories that they may have, but remember that, as in a court of law, as far as you're concerned this is only hearsay evidence, not your own first-hand experience.

Equally, you may have contact with a psychic, a medium or a spiritual leader who has definite views on your past lives. Obviously you must put such trust in this person as you think he or she deserves. On the whole, however, I feel that you are your own best judge. The point of this exercise is to encourage you to do a little self-communion. Even if you come up with no definite conclusions, the journey will have been worthwhile.

If, among your acquaintances, there are one or two people with whom you have a distinct rapport (for good or bad), you can use these relationships as points of departure for another mental trip into the past. Using your own imagination, as well as the astrological advice in this book, you can try to discern what kind of Key Lives they have in their past – and therefore what karma you may have between you.

6. Sexuality. There are sections in Chapter Seven to help you decide which sex you were in your last life – and perhaps which sex you'll be in your life to come. But you can meditate on this matter, too. Bear in mind that the purpose of having a particular sexual identity is a psychological rather than simply a procreative one. It shapes your aims and outlook more than any other factor. Sometimes it confirms your temperament, sometimes it adds piquancy to your life by conflicting with your overall character.

If you feel deeply secure in your own sexuality, without doubts or neuroses, then you've probably been that sex for a number of lives. If you recognize an ambivalence in your nature, you may well have just changed, or be about to change. This applies particularly if you're a man with a psyche that's dominant over your spirit; and, if you're a woman, with a spirit stronger than your psyche.

Equally you may have visions of yourself as a person of the opposite sex. This is one of the most powerful and common insights that a person can have of a former incarnation.

7. Occupation and Lifestyle. You may have an inner conjecture that you were a soldier, a whore, a scientist or whatever in a previous life. If this is supported by astrological evidence in Chapters Seven and Eight, you may well have discovered an important truth about yourself.

The usual precautions apply. Treat with deep suspicion any thought that you were a celebrity or held a unique post in government or saved the world from a second Black Death. Weigh in your mind how this putative former occupation relates to your present life and work. Are you simply compensating, in a fanciful way, for an inadequacy in your life today? Or is there a structural link between your work then and now? Does the one kind of job have a relevance to, or contrast with, the other one?

Don't force any glimpses of this kind to be more significant than they really are. Quite possibly you are so deeply embedded in this life that you will never have any links with the past. Don't despair – there's still astrology to help.

Using Astrology

The remainder of this book is designed to help you discover fragments, at least, of your Dramarathon to date.

The process is quite simple. Follow the rules in Chapter Six for working out your own horoscope. You are directed to the appropriate sections in later chapters for the actual interpretations that apply to you. Read these with commonsense and goodwill. Then, in Chapter 11, I show how some complete horoscopes can be pieced together to make a credible picture of one's past and present lives.

CHAPTER SIX

Figuring it Out

For most of you the biggest drawback to astrology is the sheer mathematical drudgery of it all. To calculate a horoscope properly you have to be adept with figures. You must learn the symbols of planets and signs, you must know how to extrapolate daily motions, and, worst of all, you must be certain that you haven't made any mistakes.

It's too darned hard for the average paperback reader, who, yearning for something simpler, turns his mind to, say, neurology of the lower Palaeozoic mammals.

To help you through this maze of numbers and hieroglyphs, I've made the process as easy as possible. All you have to do is add, subtract and write down the result. If you can't do that, it's clear that you weren't Isaac Newton in your last life.

To discover, with the help of astrology, who you really were, you are now going to work out the position in the sky of the Sun and Moon, Saturn, Uranus, Neptune and Pluto, plus the East Point and the Node, at the time of your birth. Because, after all, this is a paperback, not a treatise, these positions will be approximate – to the nearest couple of degrees, except for the Moon which may be out by even more, perhaps as much as seven or eight degrees. If you want more accurate positions, you must get hold of an astrological ephemeris, or ask an astrologer friend to work them out for you, or, better still, complete the application form at the back of this book for your full personal report.

Degrees in astrology, by the way, are not academic qualifications but little sections of the Zodiac – the great band of the heavens that circles our earth day after day. There are 360 degrees in the whole circle. To get an idea of the size of a degree, look at the Full Moon which is half a degree in width.

As you know, the Zodiac is divided another way in twelve equal-sized Zodiac signs, so obviously there are 30 degrees in Aries, Taurus and so forth round to Pisces.

You have four tasks facing you:

1. Zodiac Positions. For the Sun and Moon you must look up the Month No. and Day No. to discover the Circle No. From this you can obtain the Circle No. of each celestial body. For the other planets and the Node, you must look up the Year No. (and sometimes Month No. as well), and from these find the appropriate Circle Nos. Finally, for the East Point, there is a special routine explained under the East Point section. Each Circle No. gives the Zodiacal degree in which that planet lies.

2. East Houses. By a simple piece of arithmetic, subtracting each Circle No. from the East Point's Circle No., you find out in which of the twelve East Houses each planet lies at birth.

3. Node Houses. Similarly you must discover in which of the twelve Node Houses each planet lies at birth.

4. Aspects. Finally you can work out whether any important aspects are formed between the outer planets (Saturn to Pluto) and the more sensitive points of your Horoscope (Sun, Moon, Node or East Point).

Follow the instructions carefully and you can't go wrong.

SUN TABLES

Instructions	*Example*
1. Look up your Sun Month No. in Table 1 below.	Edward Kennedy, born Feb 22 Month No. for February = 311
2. Put down your date of birth (ie, between 1st and 31st)	born 22nd = 22
3. Add these together.	311 + 22 = 333
4. If total is more than 359, subtract 360.	

This is your SUN Circle Number. Enter it in the appropriate box in Tables 15 (p. 85) and 16 (p. 88). Now look up your Sun-sign in Table 2 on p. 69 and read the appropriate interpretation.

Table 1: Sun Month No.

Month	No.	Month	No.	Month	No.
Jan	279	May	39	Sep	158
Feb	311	Jun	69	Oct	187
Mar	339	Jul	98	Nov	218
Apr	10	Aug	128	Dec	248

₂₄
2 4 8
———
2 7 2

Table 2: Sun-Signs

Sun Circle No. between	Sun-Sign is	Interpretation on pages
0 and 29	Aries	92 to 95
30 and 59	Taurus	95 to 98
60 and 89	Gemini	98 to 101
90 and 119	Cancer	101 to 104
120 and 149	Leo	104 to 107
150 and 179	Virgo	108 to 111
180 and 209	Libra	111 to 114
210 and 239	Scorpio	114 to 117
240 and 269	Sagittarius	117 to 120
270 and 299	Capricorn	120 to 123
300 and 329	Aquarius	123 to 125
330 and 359	Pisces	125 to 128

MOON TABLES

Instructions

Example

1. Look at Moon Month Tables in Table 3 on pp. 71-3). Years of birth from 1900 to 1984 are shown in the left-hand column. Months of birth are shown along the top. You will find your Month No. where these two intersect.

Edward Kennedy born February 22 1932

Month No. (intersection of 1932 and Feb)   = 232

2. Look up Day No. for date of birth in Table 4 on p. 73.

Day No. (for 22nd)   = 290

3. Add these numbers together.

232 + 290   = 522

4. Optional. Depending on
   your continent of birth,
   add or subtract the
   number shown below:
   Born in

Africa (East/South)	−2
Africa (West)	0
Australia (West)	−4
Australia (East)	−5
Europe (West/North)	0
Europe (East)	−1
Far East	−4
India/Pakistan	−3
Middle East	−1
New Zealand	−6
South America	+2
South-East Asia	−4
USA/Canada (East)	+3
USA/Canada (West)	+4

Yes, Kennedy born
in Eastern USA
so 522 + 3   = 525

5. Optional. Depending on
   your time of birth, add or
   subtract the number
   shown:

Midnight–12.59 a.m.	−6
1 a.m.–2.59 a.m.	−5
3 a.m.–4.59 a.m.	−4
5 a.m.–6.59 a.m.	−3
7 a.m.–8.59 a.m.	−2
9 a.m.–10.59 a.m.	−1
11 a.m.–12.59 a.m.	0
1 p.m.–2.59 p.m.	+1
3 p.m.–4.59 p.m.	+2
5 p.m.–6.59 p.m.	+3
7 p.m.–8.59 p.m.	+4
9 p.m.–10.59 p.m.	+5
11 p.m.–11.59 p.m.	+6

Yes, Kennedy born
at 3.58 a.m.
.... so 525 − 4   = 521

6. If total is more than 359, subtract 360.

Yes, more than 359 here so
521 – 360   = 161

This gives your MOON Circle Number. Enter it in the appropriate boxes in Tables 15 (p. 85) and 16 (p. 88). Now look up your Moon-sign in Table 5 on p. 74 and read the appropriate interpretation.

Table 3: Moon Month No.

Year	Jan	Feb	Mar	Apr	May	Jun	Jul	Aug	Sep	Oct	Nov	Dec
1900	270	319	328	17	52	100	135	184	232	267	316	342
1901	40	89	98	146	181	229	264	313	2	37	86	121
1902	169	217	226	274	310	358	34	83	132	167	215	250
1903	298	346	355	44	80	129	164	213	261	296	344	19
1904	68	116	139	187	223	271	306	354	43	78	127	162
1905	211	260	268	316	351	40	75	124	173	208	257	292
1906	340	28	37	85	120	169	205	254	303	338	26	61
1907	109	157	166	215	251	299	335	23	71	106	154	190
1908	238	287	309	359	34	82	117	165	213	249	298	333
1909	22	70	79	127	162	210	246	294	343	19	68	103
1910	151	199	208	256	291	340	16	65	113	149	197	231
1911	279	328	337	26	61	110	146	194	242	277	325	0
1912	49	98	120	169	204	252	287	336	24	59	108	144
1913	193	241	250	298	333	21	56	105	154	190	238	274
1914	322	9	18	66	102	151	186	236	284	319	7	42
1915	90	138	147	196	232	281	316	5	53	88	136	171
1916	220	269	291	340	15	63	98	146	195	230	279	315
1917	3	51	60	108	143	192	227	276	325	1	49	84
1918	132	180	189	237	272	321	357	46	95	130	178	213
1919	261	309	318	7	43	92	127	175	223	258	307	342
1920	31	80	102	150	186	234	269	317	5	41	90	126
1921	174	222	231	279	314	362	38	87	136	171	220	255
1922	303	351	0	48	83	132	168	217	265	300	348	23
1923	71	120	129	178	214	262	298	346	34	69	117	153
1924	201	250	273	321	356	44	79	128	176	212	261	296
1925	345	33	42	90	125	173	209	257	307	342	31	66
1926	113	161	170	219	254	303	339	28	76	111	159	194
1927	242	291	300	349	24	73	108	157	205	240	288	323
1928	12	61	83	132	167	215	250	298	347	23	72	107

Year	Jan	Feb	Mar	Apr	May	June	Jul	Aug	Sep	Oct	Nov	Dec
1929	155	203	212	260	295	344	19	68	117	153	201	236
1930	284	332	341	29	65	114	150	198	247	282	330	5
1931	53	102	111	160	195	244	279	327	15	50	99	134
1932	183	232	254	302	337	25	61	109	158	193	242	278
1933	326	14	23	71	106	154	190	239	288	324	12	47
1934	95	143	151	200	236	285	320	9	57	92	140	175
1935	224	272	281	330	6	55	90	138	186	221	270	305
1936	354	43	65	115	148	196	231	280	329	4	53	88
1937	137	185	194	242	277	325	1	50	99	134	183	217
1938	265	313	322	11	47	96	131	180	228	263	311	346
1939	34	83	92	141	177	225	260	308	357	32	80	116
1940	165	213	235	284	319	7	42	91	139	175	224	259
1941	307	255	4	52	87	136	172	221	270	305	353	28
1942	76	124	133	182	217	266	302	350	39	74	122	157
1943	205	254	263	312	347	36	71	119	167	202	251	287
1944	336	24	46	94	129	177	213	261	310	346	35	70
1945	118	166	175	223	258	307	342	32	80	116	164	199
1946	246	295	304	352	28	77	113	161	209	244	292	327
1947	16	65	74	123	158	207	242	290	338	13	62	98
1948	146	195	217	265	300	348	23	72	121	157	205	241
1949	289	337	345	33	69	118	153	202	251	286	334	9
1950	57	105	114	163	199	248	283	332	20	55	103	138
1951	187	236	245	294	329	17	52	100	148	184	233	268
1952	317	5	28	76	111	159	194	243	292	327	16	51
1953	99	147	156	204	239	288	324	13	62	97	145	180
1954	228	276	285	334	10	59	94	143	191	226	274	309
1955	358	45	55	104	140	188	223	271	319	355	44	79
1956	128	176	198	246	281	329	5	54	103	138	187	222
1957	270	318	327	15	50	99	135	184	232	268	316	350
1958	39	87	96	145	180	229	265	313	1	36	84	120
1959	168	217	226	275	310	358	33	82	130	165	214	250
1960	299	347	9	57	92	140	175	224	273	309	358	33
1961	81	128	137	185	221	270	306	355	43	78	126	161
1962	209	258	267	316	351	40	76	124	172	207	255	290
1963	339	28	37	86	121	169	204	252	301	336	25	61
1964	109	158	180	228	263	311	346	35	84	120	168	203
1965	251	299	308	356	32	81	117	165	214	249	297	332
1966	20	68	77	126	162	211	246	294	346	17	66	101
1967	150	199	208	256	292	340	15	63	111	147	196	231
1968	280	328	350	38	73	121	157	206	255	291	339	14
1969	62	110	119	167	203	252	287	336	25	60	108	143

Year	Jan	Feb	Mar	Apr	May	Jun	Jul	Aug	Sep	Oct	Nov	Dec
1970	191	239	248	297	333	22	57	105	153	188	236	272
1971	321	10	19	67	102	150	185	234	282	318	7	42
1972	91	139	161	209	244	292	328	17	66	101	150	185
1973	232	280	289	338	13	62	98	147	195	230	278	313
1974	1	50	59	108	144	192	228	276	324	359	47	83
1975	132	180	189	238	273	321	356	44	93	129	178	213
1976	262	310	331	19	54	103	139	188	237	272	320	355
1977	43	91	100	149	184	233	269	318	6	41	89	124
1978	172	221	230	279	314	3	38	86	134	169	218	254
1979	302	351	0	48	84	132	167	215	264	299	348	24
1980	72	120	142	190	225	274	309	358	47	83	131	166
1981	214	262	271	319	355	44	80	128	177	212	260	294
1982	343	32	41	90	125	174	209	257	305	340	29	64
1983	113	162	171	219	254	302	337	26	74	110	159	195
1984	243	291	313	1	36	84	120	169	218	253	302	336

Table 4: Moon Day No.

Date of birth	Moon Day No.	Date of birth	Moon Day No.	Date of birth	Moon Day No.
1st	13	11th	145	21st	277
2nd	26	12th	158	22nd	290
3rd	40	13th	171	23rd	303
4th	53	14th	184	24th	316
5th	66	15th	198	25th	329
6th	79	16th	211	26th	343
7th	92	17th	224	27th	356
8th	105	18th	237	28th	9
9th	119	19th	250	29th	22
10th	132	20th	264	30th	35
				31st	48

Table 5: Moon-Signs

Moon Circle No. between	Moon-Sign is	Interpretation on pages
0 and 29	Aries	129 to 135
30 and 59	Taurus	135 to 140
60 and 89	Gemini	140 to 145
90 and 119	Cancer	145 to 150
120 and 149	Leo	151 to 156
150 and 179	Virgo	156 to 162
180 and 209	Libra	162 to 167
210 and 239	Scorpio	167 to 173
240 and 269	Sagittarius	173 to 179
270 and 299	Capricorn	179 to 184
300 and 329	Aquarius	185 to 190
330 and 359	Pisces	190 to 195

SATURN TABLES

Instructions	*Example*
1. Look up your Saturn Year No. in Table 6 on p. 75.	Kennedy, born 1932 Saturn Month No. = 295
2. Now see what your Saturn Month No. is from Table 7 on p. 75.	Kennedy, born February Saturn Month No. = 1
3. Add these together.	109 + 0 = 296

This is your SATURN Circle Number. Enter it in the appropriate boxes in Tables 15 (p. 85) and 16 (p. 88).

Table 6: Saturn Year No.

Year	No.	Year	No.	Year	No.	Year	No.
1900	256	1925	217	1950	163	1975	106
1901	274	1926	226	1951	175	1976	118
1902	289	1927	238	1952	187	1977	123
1903	298	1928	250	1953	199	1978	135
1904	310	1929	262	1954	211	1979	147
1905	322	1930	271	1955	223	1980	159
1906	334	1931	283	1956	232	1981	184
1907	346	1932	295	1957	244	1982	196
1908	358	1933	304	1958	256	1983	208
1909	10	1934	316	1959	268	1984	220
1910	25	1935	328	1960	280		
1911	34	1936	340	1961	289		
1912	49	1937	352	1962	301		
1913	64	1938	4	1963	313		
1914	76	1939	16	1964	322		
1915	91	1940	31	1965	331		
1916	103	1941	43	1966	343		
1917	115	1942	58	1967	2		
1918	130	1943	70	1968	15		
1919	142	1944	85	1969	27		
1920	154	1945	97	1970	40		
1921	169	1946	112	1971	55		
1922	183	1947	124	1972	67		
1923	195	1948	136	1973	82		
1924	207	1949	150	1974	94		

Table 7: Saturn Month No.

Month	No.	Month	No.	Month	No.
Jan	0	May	4	Sep	8
Feb	1	Jun	5	Oct	9
Mar	2	Jul	6	Nov	10
Apr	3	Aug	7	Dec	11

URANUS TABLES

Instructions

1. Look up your Uranus
   Year No. in Table 8
   below.

Example

Kennedy, born 1932
Uranus Year No.   = 19

This is your URANUS Circle Number. Enter it in the appropriate boxes in Tables 15 (p. 85) and 16 (p. 88).

Table 8: Uranus Year No.

Year	No.	Year	No.	Year	No.	Year	No.
1900	251	1921	336	1942	60	1963	154
1901	256	1922	339	1943	63	1964	160
1902	258	1923	342	1944	66	1965	163
1903	264	1924	348	1945	72	1966	169
1904	267	1925	352	1946	75	1967	172
1905	270	1926	355	1947	81	1968	178
1906	276	1927	0	1948	84	1969	181
1907	279	1928	3	1949	90	1970	187
1908	282	1929	6	1950	94	1971	193
1909	288	1930	12	1951	99	1972	196
1910	291	1931	15	1952	102	1973	202
1911	294	1932	19	1953	108	1974	205
1912	300	1933	24	1954	111	1975	211
1913	303	1934	27	1955	118	1976	216
1914	309	1935	30	1956	121	1977	219
1915	312	1936	36	1957	124	1978	225
1916	315	1937	39	1958	130	1979	228
1917	318	1938	42	1959	136	1980	233
1918	324	1939	48	1960	139	1981	238
1919	327	1940	51	1961	145	1982	241
1920	330	1941	57	1962	148	1983	244

Year	No.	Year	No.	Year	No.
1984	250	1986	256	1988	265
1985	253	1987	262	1989	271

NEPTUNE TABLES

Instructions	*Example*

1. Look up your Neptune   Kennedy, born 1932
   Year No. in Table 9 below.   Neptune Year No.   = 157

This is your NEPTUNE Circle Number. Enter it in the appropriate boxes in Tables 15 (p. 85) and 16 (p. 88).

Table 9: Neptune Year No.

Year	No.	Year	No.	Year	No.	Year	No.
1900	85	1919	126	1938	170	1957	211
1901	87	1920	129	1939	172	1958	214
1902	90	1921	131	1940	174	1959	216
1903	92	1922	134	1941	176	1960	218
1904	94	1923	136	1942	178	1961	220
1905	97	1924	138	1943	180	1962	222
1906	100	1925	141	1944	182	1963	224
1907	102	1926	143	1945	184	1964	226
1908	104	1927	145	1946	186	1965	228
1909	106	1928	147	1947	188	1966	230
1910	108	1929	150	1948	191	1967	232
1911	110	1930	152	1949	193	1968	234
1912	112	1931	154	1950	195	1969	236
1913	114	1932	157	1951	197	1970	238
1914	116	1933	160	1952	199	1971	240
1915	118	1934	162	1953	201	1972	242
1916	120	1935	164	1954	204	1973	245
1917	122	1936	166	1955	207	1974	247
1918	124	1937	168	1956	209	1975	249

Year	No.	Year	No.	Year	No.	Year	No.
1976	250	1980	261	1984	271	1988	278
1977	252	1981	264	1985	272	1989	280
1978	255	1982	266	1986	274		
1979	258	1983	268	1987	276		

PLUTO TABLES

Instructions	*Example*
1. Simply look up your Pluto Year No. in Table 10 below.	Kennedy, born 1932 Pluto Year No. = 111

This is your PLUTO Circle Number. Enter it in the appropriate boxes in Tables 15 (p. 85) and 16 (p. 88).

Table 10: Pluto Year No.

Year	No.	Year	No.	Year	No.	Year	No.
1900	75	1916	92	1932	111	1948	134
1901	77	1917	93	1933	113	1949	136
1902	78	1918	95	1934	114	1950	137
1903	79	1919	96	1935	115	1951	139
1904	80	1920	97	1936	117	1952	140
1905	81	1921	98	1937	118	1953	142
1906	82	1922	99	1938	119	1954	144
1907	83	1923	100	1939	121	1955	145
1908	84	1924	101	1940	122	1956	148
1909	85	1925	103	1941	123	1957	150
1910	86	1926	104	1942	125	1958	152
1911	87	1927	105	1943	126	1959	153
1912	88	1928	106	1944	128	1960	155
1913	89	1929	107	1945	129	1961	157
1914	90	1930	109	1946	131	1962	159
1915	91	1931	110	1947	132	1963	161

Year	No.	Year	No.	Year	No.	Year	No.
1964	163	1971	178	1978	196	1985	214
1965	165	1972	181	1979	198	1986	216
1966	168	1973	183	1980	199	1987	218
1967	170	1974	185	1981	201	1988	221
1968	172	1975	188	1982	204	1989	224
1969	174	1976	190	1983	207		
1970	176	1977	193	1984	210		

NODE TABLES

Instructions	*Example*
1. Look up your Node Year No. in Table 11 below.	Kennedy, born 1932 Node Year No. = 341
2. Look up your Node Month No. in Table 12 on p. 80.	Kennedy, born February Node Month No. = 18
3. Add these together.	341 + 18 = 359
4. If total is more than 359, subtract 360.	

This is your NODE Circle Number. Enter it in the appropriate boxes in Tables 15 (p. 85) and 16 (p. 88).

Table 11: Node Year No.

Year	No.	Year	No.	Year	No.	Year	No.
1900	240	1909	66	1918	252	1927	77
1901	220	1910	46	1919	232	1928	58
1902	201	1911	27	1920	213	1929	39
1903	182	1912	8	1921	194	1930	20
1904	162	1913	348	1922	174	1931	0
1905	143	1914	329	1923	155	1932	341
1906	124	1915	310	1924	136	1933	322
1907	104	1916	290	1925	116	1934	302
1908	85	1917	271	1926	97	1935	283

Year	No.	Year	No.	Year	No.	Year	No.
1936	264	1949	12	1962	121	1975	229
1937	244	1950	353	1963	101	1976	210
1938	225	1951	333	1964	82	1977	191
1939	206	1952	314	1965	63	1978	171
1940	186	1953	295	1966	43	1979	152
1941	167	1954	275	1967	24	1980	133
1942	147	1955	256	1968	5	1981	113
1943	128	1956	237	1969	345	1982	94
1944	109	1957	217	1970	326	1983	75
1945	89	1958	198	1971	307	1984	56
1946	70	1959	179	1972	287	1985	6
1947	51	1960	159	1973	268		
1948	31	1961	140	1974	249		

Table 12: Node Month No.

Month	No.	Month	No.	Month	No.
Jan	20	May	13	Sep	7
Feb	18	Jun	12	Oct	5
Mar	16	Jul	10	Nov	2
Apr	15	Aug	8	Dec	0

EAST POINT TABLES

Instructions	*Example*
1. You can work out your East Point only if you know your time of birth. First you must substract an hour for summer time if you were born in Britain between, roughly, late March and early October. Subtract an hour, too, if you were born during World War II. If you are not sure about summer time in your country of birth, consult your local reference library.	
2. Write down your Sun Circle No. calculated earlier on p. 68.	Kennedy Circle No. = 333
3. Add 360.	333 + 360 = 693
4. Look up your Time No. in Table 13 on pp. 82–3, where your hour of birth (a.m. or p.m.) intersects with the nearest minute of birth.	Kennedy, born 3.58 a.m. so 3 a.m. intersects with 55 min = −121
5. Add or subtract, as indicated.	693 − 121 = 572

Instructions	*Example*

6. Optional. Make allowance for your longitude of birth compared with your Standard Meridian. In Britain the Standard Meridian is 0. Look up your longitude of birth in an atlas, and see the difference east or west of your Standard Meridian. Add this difference for east but subtract the difference if west.

Kennedy born Boston in Eastern Time Zone where Standard Meridian is 75 W. Boston = 71 W, so Boston is 4 degrees east of the Standard Meridian.
So 4 + 572   = 576

7. Subtract 270.

so 576 – 270   = 306

8. If total is greater than 359 subtract another 360.

This is your EAST POINT No. Enter it in the appropriate box in Table 15 (p. 85).

Table 13: Time No

Hours a.m.	0	5	10	15	20	25	30	35	40	45	50	55
12	-180	-179	-177	-176	-175	-174	-173	-171	-170	-169	-168	-166
1	-165	-164	-162	-161	-160	-159	-158	-156	-155	-154	-153	-151
2	-150	-149	-147	-146	-145	-144	-143	-141	-140	-139	-138	-138
3	-135	-134	-132	-131	-130	-129	-128	-126	-125	-124	-123	-121
4	-120	-119	-117	-116	-115	-114	-113	-111	-110	-109	-108	-106
5	-105	-104	-102	-101	-100	-99	-98	-96	-95	-94	-93	-91
6	-90	-89	-87	-86	-85	-84	-83	-81	-80	-79	-78	-76
7	-75	-74	-72	-71	-70	-69	-68	-66	-65	-64	-63	-61
8	-60	-59	-57	-56	-55	-54	-53	-51	-50	-49	-48	-46
9	-45	-44	-42	-41	-40	-39	-38	-36	-35	-34	-33	-31
10	-30	-29	-27	-26	-25	-24	-23	-21	-20	-19	-18	-16
11	-15	-14	-12	-11	-10	-9	-8	-6	-5	-4	-3	-1

Minutes

Hours					Minutes						
p.m.	**0**	**5**	**10**	**15**	**20**	**25**	**30**	**35**	**40**	**45**	**50**	**55**
12	0	1	3	4	5	6	8	9	10	11	12	14
1	15	16	18	19	20	21	23	24	25	26	27	29
2	30	31	33	34	35	36	38	39	40	41	42	44
3	45	46	48	49	50	51	53	54	55	56	57	59
4	60	61	63	64	65	66	68	69	70	71	72	74
5	75	76	78	79	80	81	83	84	85	86	87	89
6	90	91	93	94	95	96	98	99	100	101	102	104
7	105	106	108	109	110	111	113	114	115	116	117	119
8	120	121	123	124	125	126	128	129	130	131	132	134
9	135	136	138	139	140	141	143	144	145	146	147	149
10	150	151	153	154	155	156	158	159	160	161	162	164
11	165	166	168	169	170	171	173	174	175	176	177	179

EAST HOUSE TABLES

Instructions

1. Follow the instructions in Table 15 on p. 85. First add 360 to your East Point. Then, in the case of the Sun, Moon and each planet, take away the Circle No. (from the new East Point (subtracting 360 if need be), to get the Angle No. Then use Table 14 on p. 84 to look up the right East House No.

2. You will find the interpretation for each East House position in Chapter 9 (Sun and Moon) and Chapter 10 (planets).

Example

Kennedy's East House Nos. are calculated in Table 15 example on p. 86.

Table 14: House Nos.

Angle No. between	East or Node House No. is
1 and 30	12th
31 and 60	11th
61 and 90	10th
91 and 120	9th
121 and 150	8th
151 and 180	7th
181 and 210	6th
211 and 240	5th
241 and 270	4th
271 and 300	3rd
301 and 330	2nd
331 and 0	1st

Table 15: East Houses

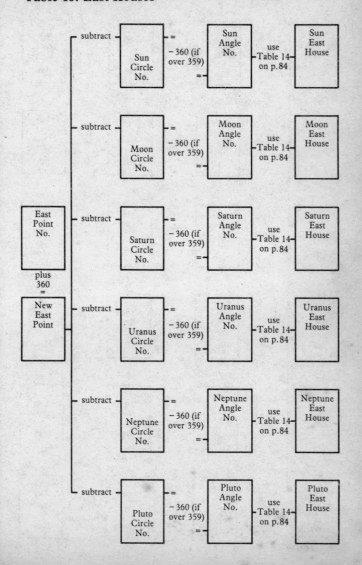

Table 15: Example of Edward Kennedy East Houses

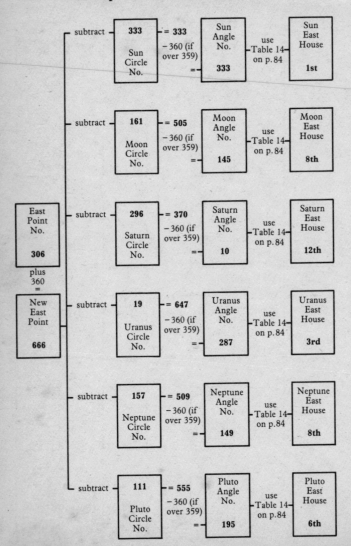

East Point No.

306

plus 360 =

New East Point

666

| subtract | 333 Sun Circle No. | = 333 – 360 (if over 359) = 333 | Sun Angle No. 333 | use Table 14 on p.84 | Sun East House 1st |

| subtract | 161 Moon Circle No. | = 505 – 360 (if over 359) = 145 | Moon Angle No. 145 | use Table 14 on p.84 | Moon East House 8th |

| subtract | 296 Saturn Circle No. | = 370 – 360 (if over 359) = 10 | Saturn Angle No. 10 | use Table 14 on p.84 | Saturn East House 12th |

| subtract | 19 Uranus Circle No. | = 647 – 360 (if over 359) = 287 | Uranus Angle No. 287 | use Table 14 on p.84 | Uranus East House 3rd |

| subtract | 157 Neptune Circle No. | = 509 – 360 (if over 359) = 149 | Neptune Angle No. 149 | use Table 14 on p.84 | Neptune East House 8th |

| subtract | 111 Pluto Circle No. | = 555 – 360 (if over 359) = 195 | Pluto Angle No. 195 | use Table 14 on p.84 | Pluto East House 6th |

NODE HOUSE TABLES

Instructions	*Example*
1. Follow the instructions laid out in Table 16 on p. 88. You use the same procedure as for East Houses: add 360 to the Node Circle No., and in each case subtract the planet's Circle No. (and 360 as well, if necessary) to find the Angle No. Use Table 14 on p. 84 to discover the appropriate Node House No.	Kennedy's Node House Nos. are calculated in Table 16 example on p. 89.
2. The interpretation of each Node House position is given in Chapter Nine (Sun and Moon) and Chapter Ten (planets).	

Table 16: Node Houses

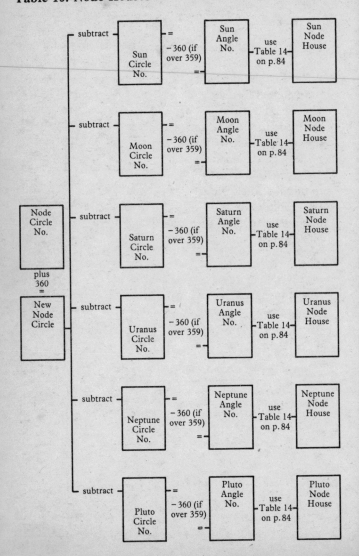

Table 16: Example of Edward Kennedy Node Houses

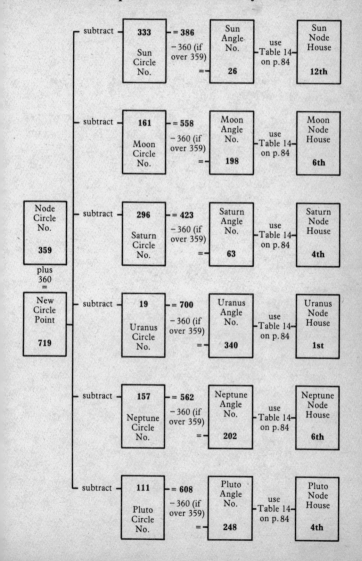

ASPECT TABLES

Instructions	*Example*

1. This is a simple check to see if there are any major aspects between each of the outer planets and the Sun, Moon or East Point.

2. Taking each planet in turn, compare its Circle No. with the Circle Nos. of the Sun, Moon and East Point. In each case, take the smaller number away from the larger one: the result is the Angle, which should be entered in Table 18 on p. 91.

   Kennedy's aspects are worked out in Table 18 example on p. 91.

3. Use Table 17 below to see if there is an aspect involved. If so, put 'yes' in the appropriate box.

4. Interpretations of these aspects are given in Chapter Ten.

Table 17: Aspect Calculations

If Angle lies between

0 and 10	
80 and 100	
170 and 190	then YES, there is an aspect
260 and 280	
350 and 359	
Otherwise,	NO aspect

Table 18: Aspectarian

	SUN		MOON		EAST POINT	
	Angle	Aspect	Angle	Aspect	Angle	Aspect
SATURN						
URANUS						
NEPTUNE						
PLUTO						

Table 18: Example of Edward Kennedy Aspectarian

	SUN		MOON		EAST POINT	
	Angle	Aspect	Angle	Aspect	Angle	Aspect
SATURN	37	No	135	No	10	Yes
URANUS	314	No	142	No	287	No
NEPTUNE	176	Yes	4	Yes	149	No
PLUTO	222	No	50	No	195	No

CHAPTER SEVEN

Spirit

In Chapter Six, FIGURING IT OUT, you were shown how to calculate the position of the Sun. This, very broadly, establishes the nature of your spirit: the kind of character you possess in this life.

There are twelve different kinds of spirit, represented by the various signs of the Zodiac. In this chapter you can look up the section referring to your spirit, according to your Sun Circle No., and learn something about your innermost character. Treat everything you read as suggestions rather than definite assertions, points of departure in your journey of self-discovery. My remarks are meant to inspire your own imagination, triggering memories buried deep within you.

Spirit in Aries: Sun 0 – 29

Your Character in this Life
Your Aries spirit is like a flamethrower, burning a path through life with great vigour. It is simple, direct and sure of itself. It brooks no arguments.

You can be a self-centred person, for it's hard for you to put your ego to one side and see life through the eyes of others. But you are not necessarily selfish in a greedy sense. You simply have strong enthusiasms that need to be satisfied.

Your Aries fire is like male sexual energy: ardent and generous at best, but obstreperous if thwarted. Certainly you can be hasty, always wanting quick results and getting steamed up with frustration if people or circumstances obstruct your progress.

At best, you are a strong, courageous type hating the idea of defeat. You are proud to be self-sufficient. You have a great respect for facts, and feel relatively ill-at-ease with guesses or theories. You live in the Here and Now, and are unhappy in the world of fantasy.

You can exert a kind of leadership – the 'follow me' variety that marches headlong into battle. Without your kind of Aries spirit, there would be no pioneers. No one to defend the innocent. No one to attack them, either.

Your Overall Development

There are several stages of Zodiacal development stretched over many lifetimes. You must decide for yourself what level you have reached.

The PRIMITIVE Ariean is totally self-centred, a victim of his own desires. His first task is to realize that, if he always rushes blindly into battle, he ends up hurt more often than his prey.

The AVERAGE Ariean faces subtler tests. He must learn imagination, putting himself in other people's shoes. He must temper his own impetuousness with caution, respect for others, and forward planning. He must learn practical skills to help him master the environment around him.

Metaphorically – and, in distant times, literally – he must move from being an animal to a hunter, from pack-leader to army commander, from flint-age man to modern engineer.

The ADVANCED Ariean can marry many of these attributes into an integrated personality, without actually snuffing them out. He can sublimate desire without losing it altogether. He can respect the pace at which others move, without slackening his own momentum. He knows he is still the leader, but he can exhort with charm and humour instead of merely exasperation. He can time his moments of intervention with great skill, knowing when to push, when to be patient.

Careers that you may have followed in the past are anything open-air, attacking, self-sufficient, where resourcefulness was called for. This will have included manual work, engineering, construction work, architecture, the armed services and certain aspects of health care: dentistry and surgery in particular.

Spiritually there are links with the samurai, Zen Buddhism, the whirling dervishes and Rome. All these were training grounds for the Ariean spirit. But equally it will have been shaped by independent experience, miles from any culture: as herdsman, farmer, gold-digger, oil-driller or camel-driver on the great trade routes of the past.

Your Sexual History

Aries is very much a male, *yang*-oriented spirit. It is expressed most clearly and forcibly through a male person; but since spiritual evolution is concerned with *modifying* inborn characteristics rather than simply indulging them, perhaps an Aries woman is making more progress than her male counterpart.

If you're a MAN now, the likelihood is that you've been a man for a number of lifetimes and that you're leading a life of continuity (see below). Another possibility is that you've just become a man after quite a spell as a woman, and are leading a second-breath life.

If you're a WOMAN now, you have probably just changed sex since your previous life. In this century of women's rights, many souls who have learnt assertiveness as a man have incarnated this time as women.

Alternatively, if you are having a life of reaction, you could have been a victimized woman in your past life who has come back with the temptation to give your former persecutor the rough edge of your Aries spirit this time round.

What kind of Life?

There are four main kinds of life that you could be leading.

A LIFE OF CONTINUITY means that you are in the midst of a long phase of Ariean development. You will have definite

Ariean skills as a leader and man of action. You'll feel self-confident and happy with your overall personality, and your great aim in life will be to contribute to the progress of the world.

A LIFE OF REACTION, on the other hand, means that you have your Aries spirit temporarily, either to pay life back for hurting you in the past or, less likely in your case, to experience for yourself conditions that you mocked or criticized in an earlier life. You could have a definite obsession about one person or lifestyle. There is the strong possibility, if you are leading this kind of life, of being born with a physical or mental defect or of being involved in a serious accident in the course of your life.

A DEAD-END LIFE means that you have reached the end – for the moment, at least – of your Aries experience. You will come face to face with the consequences of the Aries spirit: that violence does not pay, that selfishness drives friends away, and that sexual conquest without love brings loneliness and lack of fulfilment. Your life may create self-hatred and self-doubts, so that you yearn to obliterate your personality and start all over again.

Finally, a SECOND-BREATH LIFE means a brand-new start, after a series of lives developing other parts of the Zodiac. You feel like bursting out with energy, joy and inventiveness, though you may not quite know what to do with it all!

Spirit in Taurus: Sun 30 – 59

Your Character in this Life

Your Taurean spirit resembles an oak tree: slow-growing, deep-rooted and difficult to transplant. It has a steady rhythm of its own, and can be put to many practical uses.

What motivates you is the desire for something solid, and lasting, be it a family or business or leisure pursuit, that acts as a kind of memorial to your existence. You stand four-square, legs planted in the everyday world, bringing life down to your ground eye-level. You gently debunk the high-falutin' type of ideas; you veer away from theories; you appreciate the down-to-earth facts of life.

You adopt proprietorial rights towards *your* possessions, *your* friends, *your* own comfy habits. You are great at maintaining an agreeable situation; but if you must adapt, then you do so slowly, at your own speed. The dinosaurs were Taureans who, sadly, adapted too slowly!

You are not a natural leader. You prefer the quiet second-in-command role where you can act as sensible balance to your hot-headed boss! You have deep sympathies for the good things in life – love, beauty and comfort – but at worst you are obstinate to the point of bloody-mindedness.

Your Overall Development

There are several stages of Zodiacal development stretched over many lifetimes. You must decide for yourself what level you have reached.

The PRIMITIVE Taurean is nothing but a suet pudding, caught up in his own comforts and too lazy to bother about other people. He is a creature of his own habits, probably a fatalist at heart, but is developing a sense of beauty and human warmth.

The AVERAGE Taurean is developing a nose for business, learning how to produce goods efficiently and conduct himself with integrity in his dealings with others. His possessiveness will be tested, for he must learn how to lose what he loves best, and still survive.

In a manner of speaking, he is changing from peasant to bourgeois, from Casanova to family man, from folk singer to opera star. In each case, he is cultivating his native gifts into great accomplishment.

The ADVANCED Taurean continues this process. He is a fine organizer, fair to everyone, constant in his affections and able to accept many responsibilities. He is still tested, of course: for smugness and complacency, and for his ability to respond quickly when by instinct he wants to take his time.

Careers that you may have followed in the past are anything steady and secure, calling for perseverance and constructive ability. This will have included manual work, many skilled crafts, farming, the property business, banking, insurance and the food and drink trade.

Spiritually there are links with Roman Catholicism, especially adoration of the Virgin Mary. There could also, long ago, have been nature worship and some link with folklore and magic. All these contributed to the development of your Taurean spirit. But equally it will have been shaped by collective social experience: within family life, working on behalf of the community.

Your Sexual History

Taurus can manifest equally well through men and women, though it is essentially a female, *yin*-oriented spirit.

If you're a MAN now, the chances are that you were probably a woman in your last life. There can often be a steady alternation between the sexes during a Taurean phase of development. This is specially likely if you're a family man at heart, and also if you have strong talent in the arts.

It's quite easy being a Taurean male, as much nowadays in our organized 20th century as earlier when most people lived on the land.

Taurus suits women. If you're a WOMAN now, you will probably have swapped and changed between the sexes with reasonable frequency in the past. To have a Taurean life as a woman is often a sign of gently good karma; you can exercise your age-old skills as a mother without fuss or moral testing.

What kind of Life?

There are four main kinds of life that you could be leading.

A LIFE OF CONTINUITY for Taureans was very common in the old days, when most people lived in tribes and rural communities. Nowadays it's going out of fashion, though souls return to Taurus every so often as a kind of refresher course in down-to-earth living.

A Taurean LIFE OF REACTION is also fairly uncommon. It could occur if you had been irresponsible in a previous life, and needed to be taught patience through restriction. Possibly, too, if you had developed a lively but mischievous mind, you might need to be encased in Taurean bovinity for a while, just to quieten you down!

A DEAD-END life is quite common among Taurean spirits in the past two centuries. Mankind has exploited Earth so mercilessly, and has been so cruel to fellow-humans in the pursuit of wealth, that many people born under Taurus are discovering the futility of a material way of life. Sometimes this happens through obesity, physical or psychological. When the body or soul becomes so bloated that it cannot breathe properly, the person is being taught the need for slimming.

SECOND-BREATH LIVES are quite common with Taurus. If people have been busy developing their minds or their spiritual aspirations, it's nice to leave the hysteria behind and start again with a plain, old-fashioned practical home-making life as a Taurean.

Spirit in Gemini: Sun 60 – 89

Your Character in this Life
Your Gemini spirit is like a spring breeze blowing hither and yon, restless and insubstantial. It will never stay still or settle down. It is forever changing direction.

You bend before this wind, preferring expediency to high principles, and you tend to wriggle out of unpleasant duties if you possibly can. Your agile, fast-moving mind can pick up the smattering of ideas in a very short time, and thereafter you're an expert in the subject – so you think! With your fluent, expressive way of talking, you can begin a sentence without knowing how it will end; and this symbolizes much of your life, for equally you can begin a career or marriage without knowing how it will develop.

This will-o'-the-wisp temperament is immensely attractive ...for a while. Then it can prove tiring in the way that any cheeky, too-clever-by-half youngster can. It is very hard for the Geminian spirit to escape from the Peter Pan outlook and grow up.

In the same way, without realizing it you can be two-faced. You are so adept at playing a multiplicity of roles that, in the end, you may not know who you really are.

Your Overall Development

There are several stages of Zodiacal development stretched over many lifetimes. You must decide for yourself what level you have reached.

The PRIMITIVE Geminian is just a naughty boy, never growing up. He cheats, lies, double-crosses and dissembles without believing he is doing wrong. His first task is to realize that if he cries 'wolf' once too often, no one will accept his word when he's really telling the truth.

The AVERAGE Geminian knows the defects of his character, and tries to do something about them. He knows that he must accept some discipline if he's to achieve anything substantial, and he attempts to put his mind to serious work. But he's always tempted to fall back on his charm, to skip the difficult bits, and fudge the issues.

His psychological journey is from schoolboy to teacher, spiv to honest trader, jokester to journalist.

The ADVANCED Geminian has wonderful gifts of speech and writing that he can use to great expressive effect. His task is to light the world with knowledge, but to do so with humility. He has outgrown the Peter Pan image, but he still faces moral tests

- in particular, the need to keep steady when surrounded by crisis. The Grand Master in chess shows the Geminian intellect at a high level; and the diplomat, manoeuvring without losing integrity, shows advanced Geminian skill at dealing with people.

Careers that you may have followed in the past are anything clever, devious, mental or communicative – from messenger, novelist, street trader or ambassador to minstrel, travelling player or acrobat.

Spiritually there are links with Tibet and Greece. In ancient days you may have learnt many occult skills that are now lying dormant in your soul. If you have any feeling for numbers, geometry and crystal-clear philosophy, you may well have had some dealings with the early Greeks.

Your Sexual History

Gemini is a neutral Zodiac sign. If it has a sexuality, it is more feminine than male. Gemini is the great cross-roads of the Zodiac, when one sex switches over to the other – or, as does happen, gets caught in between.

In other ways, Geminians often have bisexual attitudes, or even none at all.

It's wrong for Geminian men to force themselves into one exclusive sexual mode (and remember that I'm talking about role-playing, not physical sex). Being born under Gemini gives you an almost unique chance to see life simultaneously from two angles.

If you're a WOMAN now, you may be slipping gently into a male-oriented soul by your next life, but not necessarily. There could be special tensions between being a Geminian and a mother, as they are somewhat incompatible. A good many women are leading lives of reaction (see below), getting their own back on men who have betrayed them in the past or, more generally, liberating themselves sexually from a series of lives spent in nunneries.

What kind of Life?

There are four main kinds of life that you could be leading.

A LIFE OF CONTINUITY means that you have been developing your Geminian spirit over a series of lives. You will have clear-cut Geminian talents – as writer, actor or musician, or perhaps mathematician – and your whole attitude to life should be joyous and positive.

A LIFE OF REACTION, on the other hand, means that you are re-entering your Geminian spirit briefly for a particular karmic purpose. You may be tempted to pay back someone who cheated you in the past; or you could be taught to treasure the independence that you considered of little worth in earlier lives.

Geminian disabilities involve the use of hands, speech or the breathing mechanism. If you have an impediment in these areas – from a lisp to asthma – you are experiencing some karma. In the past you could have prevented the truth from being spoken, for instance.

A DEAD-END LIFE means that you have reached a cul-de-sac in your Geminian path of development. You cannot evade any longer: to progress further, you must turn your back on the less happy side of your nature. You may dislike being a Geminian very much. You may hate being so two-faced and unreliable. And you may yearn, as a result of your experiences, to be a more responsible and grown-up soul in the future.

Finally, a SECOND-BREATH LIFE, which is very common for Gemini, means a brand-new start after a series of disagreeable experiences elsewhere in the Zodiac. Gemini is a lovely holiday-centre, where souls can rest and recuperate after a lot of fighting in the Scorpio battle-zone!

Spirit in Cancer: Sun 90 – 119

Your Character in this Life

Your Cancer spirit is like a bubbling country river: flowing where it feels wanted, providing the psychological moisture that encourages healthy growth. Sometimes it gushes too much – with great floods of sentimentality or self-pity. Always it flows towards the great sea of the Unconscious.

The great paradox of your spirit is that you want to be a busy, practical person at an everyday level, but are really an introvert with a highly sensitive inner nature that can easily be hurt.

Home and family are your natural ambience. You regard the past as the womb from which the present has emerged – and in thoughts and plans, and as a source of inspiration, you look back to the past rather than forward to the future. At heart, you're an emotional conservative.

In your moral outlook on life, you are susceptible to short-term pressure but remarkably tenacious on matters of principle. Your most difficult test in life is knowing how tightly your motherly apron-strings should be tied around your 'children' – which may be real children, or a job of work, an ideal, a collection of treasured objects, a garden, or a few close cronies that you have made into your 'family'.

Think again of a river. It seems to have no will of its own, easily diverted by a dam or a twist of landscape. Yet it still reaches the distant sea. The spirit of Cancer, which seems such an easy push, has a lot of pull of its own!

Your Overall Development

There are several stages of Zodiacal development stretched over many lifetimes. You must decide for yourself what level you have reached.

The PRIMITIVE Cancerian is highly emotional and panicky, clinging to any kind of emotional security it can find and, like a vampire, sucking vitality from others. He will attract attention through hysterics and an over-active imagination. In turn, he will 'mother' whatever takes his fancy in a ridiculously over-possessive way.

The AVERAGE Cancerian is still searching for emotional peace, but is taking a more sensible, controlled path towards it.

He is liberating himself from over-dependence on others, learning how to let his 'children' go, and is starting to put his imagination to good creative use.

Metaphorically, he is developing from child to parent, from orphan to do-gooder, from clansman to citizen of the world.

Finally, the ADVANCED Cancerian has great soulfulness. With his emotional power he can touch many hearts, and can spread a feeling of togetherness among a wide group of people. He knows by experience when to apply and release this power for the good of all. He is a creative person in the widest sense of the word: creative in human relations, in the arts, and in making people feel wholesome again.

Careers that you may have followed in the past are any jobs that help other people – teaching, charity work, shopkeeping and all kinds of business.

Spiritually there are links with Catholicism, Judaism and the Egyptian mystery temples. All these have been training grounds for the Cancerian spirit. But equally it will have been shaped by much family life, and as nurse, cook, gardener or any other domestic work.

Your Sexual History

Cancer is very much a female, *yin*-oriented spirit. It is expressed most powerfully through a woman's soul; but it is also the most effective means in spiritual evolution for teaching men how to be soft, passive and inner-directed.

If you're a MAN now, you are probably on the point of switch-over to the other sex, but not necessarily. Being a Cancerian male is one of the most difficult tasks in the whole Zodiac. You are constantly balancing your needs as a macho male with the soft-centred Cancerian nature.

But you have a special role at present, helping the world to become more responsive to *yin* qualities. You, more than most men, are prepared to accept women as equals.

If you're a WOMAN now, your spirit is occupying one of the

more congenial parts of the Zodiac. You can enjoy your roles as wife and mother, and in addition can play a busy, practical role in the outer world. Most satisfying.

What kind of Life?
There are four main kinds of life that you could be leading.

A LIFE OF CONTINUITY means that you're in the middle of a sustained bout of Cancerian development. This is more likely if you're a woman than a man – though, to be honest, if you are leading this kind of placid, motherly existence through a series of lives, you could be swopping from one sex to the other.

A LIFE OF REACTION, on the other hand, means that you're spending probably a single life as a Cancerian, simply as a bounce-back from a very different lifestyle beforehand. If you're a tough Cancerian, you could have come back for revenge against someone who ran away from you in the past. If you're thin-skinned, you are suffering the same kind of pains and problems that you inflicted on people in an earlier incarnation.

If you feel you have reached a DEAD-END LIFE, you could come face to face with the consequences of Cancerian hysteria: madness, emotional abandon, loneliness because your precious children have flown the nest. But because Cancer is perhaps the most basic and sustaining of Zodiacal paths of development, there is really no dead-end involved: you simply return over and over again, learning how to control your emotional nature.

Finally, Cancer provides quite a large proportion of SECOND-BREATH LIVES. It's such a nice, restful, homely temperament to return to, after a strained spell elsewhere in the Zodiac.

Spirit in Leo: Sun 120 – 149

Your Character in this Life
Your Leo spirit is like the sun itself: radiant, powerful and

exhibitionist! At its best, it's the most glorious thing in sight; but a single grey cloud can soon obliterate its warmth.

At your worst, you come across too strongly, like the sun at noon. But although you enjoy power and position, you do not like to fight for your authority. You prefer to be king rather than prime minister, and much prefer to win your rewards than earn your due deserts.

At the root of your Leo spirit is your pride. It is a strong, confident self-assurance at the best of times. But you can plunge into sudden depressions, and you lack natural inner resources to cope with real difficulties. If anyone can die of a broken heart, it is Leo.

Leos are born to be king, so they think – but there are many different kinds of monarch: the spiv emperor (like Amin of Uganda); the heroic figure-head (like Henry V of Agincourt); or the constitutional king, the soul whose duty has conquered his pride.

You need to live in a constant aura of affection. So long as you are surrounded by love and attention, you're as radiant and golden as the Sun!

Your Overall Development

There are several stages of Zodiacal development stretched over many lifetimes. You must decide for yourself what level you have reached.

The PRIMITIVE Leonian is full of vain glory: absurdly pretentious, expecting everything his own way. He is a boastful character, and what he cannot get by charm, he grabs by force.

The AVERAGE Leonian tries to tame his nature to suit the world about him. He accepts that egotism has its limits, though he still finds it hard to be truly humble. He is good at organizing others, winning their support rather than cowing them into obedience. But he does have difficulty in attending to little details, and must learn to love as generously as he demands from others.

He's in the process, over many lives, of moving from the braggart to the prince, from little bitch to show business star, from barrack-room lawyer to high court judge.

Finally, the ADVANCED Leonian can be a noble human spirit. He has great personal charisma, so that people flock to be near him. He has true powers of leadership, able to inspire their souls to his own vision of what life is all about. He can conquer the Leo faults, avoiding favouritism and the need for personal glory; but he is still tested – for example, in seeing something beautiful destroyed, yet starting to recreate it all over again.

Careers that you may have followed in the past are anything calling for authority, where you could exercise control over others, and involving some degree of luxuriance and dignity. This could have been goldsmith, jeweller, helping to run a palace, make fine clothes or get people to enjoy themselves in sport and entertainment.

Spiritually there are links with the Aztecs and Minoan cultures, aspects of Greek and Roman religious life (especially in the worship of Apollo). But the Leo spirit can be shaped by humbler influences: the fun of the theatre, the joy of romance, the pleasure of little children.

Your Sexual History

Leo is meant to be a male Zodiac sign, but truthfully it is the spirit of the senses; and women, perhaps better than men, can embody the dignity, the warm-heartedness of this midsummer sign.

If you're a MAN now, you are cultivating some fine Leo qualities: a sense of honour, camaraderie, the ability to attract women. If you feel you possess these virtues in abundance, you may well have been a Leo person for quite a few lives. But whereas Leo women can get away with vanity, Leo men cannot – so this is the main fault to be eradicated.

The likelihood is that you're in the midst of a series of male incarnations.

If you're a WOMAN now, you've probably just changed sex in this life. This is specially true if you're a bit of a tomboy at heart. If, on the other hand, you feel quite secure in your femininity, you're probably in the middle of a womanly phase – though not necessarily always as a Leonian.

What kind of Life?

There are four main kinds of life that you could be leading.

It will be a LIFE OF CONTINUITY if you feel happy and secure within your Leo spirit. It's a mistake to think that people are increasingly Leo the longer you remain in this sign. On the contrary, the more Leonian experience you have, the better able you are to integrate with the rest of the Zodiac. So the more mixed your overall horoscope, the more likely that you're leading this kind of life.

A LIFE OF REACTION, on the other hand, is equally probable. Spiritual evolution is much concerned with the central task facing the Leo spirit: the wise use of love. Souls who have been the victims of love in the past may incarnate quickly as a Leonian – either to pay their tormentor back with a dose of the same medicine or, more hopefully, to learn to rise above the situation.

A DEAD-END Leo life is possible but rare in the modern world. It would be a life where you see, perhaps for the first time, the full horror of your inflated ego. If you are having one romantic setback after another, and if you are heartily sick of your vain, pompous ways, you may indeed be lancing the Leo boil once and for all.

There's no doubt that a SECOND-BREATH life is quite frequent under Leo. It's such a bonny sign for a holiday. Identify yourself with this type of life if you are popular and full of high spirits, and feel as though an unpleasant experience is now behind you. In this life you are simply wearing the Leo spirit as a refreshing change from more serious attire.

Spirit in Virgo: Sun 150 – 179

Your Character in this Life

Your Virgo spirit resembles the sea lapping a beach: never-ending in its work, a bit monotonous after a while, but sparkling fresh, washing everything clean again.

You keep a sharp, critical eye on everything, including yourself. You inquire, you question, you seek to improve. Indeed, you see life as a perpetual series of tasks to be tackled – some pleasant, others arduous, but all of them necessary.

You are recognized as a quiet, undemonstrative type who is happier working in the backroom than enjoying the glory and prestige of personal acclaim. Often you can be self-conscious, particularly in situations where you feel unsure of yourself. If you have any egotism, it takes the form of mental arrogance; you like to think that you know best – a subtle way of criticizing others!

At times you seem to erect a psychological plate-glass window between yourself and reality. You're there, but people can't get close to you. You adopt a cautious, wait-and-see attitude towards new acquaintances.

You care about moral questions, being an idealist at heart. But you marry this desire for purity with a sensible, down-to-earth pragmatism that prevents you from going to silly extremes.

Your Overall Development

There are several stages of Zodiacal development stretched over many lifetimes. You must decide for yourself what level you have reached.

The PRIMITIVE Virgoan sees only the flaws in a scheme, never its possibilities. He never praises anyone, dislikes the conditions in which he finds himself, and seems constantly irritable and discontented. His horizon is bounded by the circle of his own duties, and he concentrates solely on the details under his nose.

The AVERAGE Virgoan has learnt to discriminate in a more kindly way. He still pigeonholes ideas – and people – in a somewhat heartless fashion, but he tries to help the community without turning into a nosey do-gooder. He still has some way to go towards his objective – service without protest – but he's making progress.

You could say that he's moving from a nagger to a constructive critic, from nit-picker to craftsman, from shrew to economist.

The ADVANCED Virgoan is a creature of high ideals and great inner purity. He follows his conscience, works happily within the community without need for personal glory, and has a shrewd intellect able to spot flaws and put them right without fuss. He radiates an air of peace, decorum and loving kindness which is most refreshing.

Careers which you may have followed in the past are almost anything, for the great Virgoan talent is turning your hand to many tasks. You tend to be better suited to brain-work than brawny occupations. Good at teaching, medicine, science, clerical work and accountancy.

Spiritually there are links with the Christian church, protestantism and almost any kind of ascetic calling. You may have spent some lives in relative solitude, others busy serving others without much complaint. But equally you could have developed your Virgoan qualities in any quiet, humdrum lifestyle: as villager, suburbanite or city-dweller on the fringes of power and excitement.

Your Sexual History

Virgo is another neutral spirit, neither male or female in orientation. Indeed, there is a constant drag towards celibacy, either voluntary or inflicted by circumstances.

If you're a MAN now, there's no way of knowing what sex

you've been in the recent past. Probably you were a man earlier if your mind is sharp, analytical and good with numbers. If you are fussy in personal habits, especially in hygiene, you may have been a woman.

Certainly your danger now is snuffing out the humanity of personal relations by being too dry and unsympathetic. Your great talent – in the 20th century in particular – is developing platonic friendships where the sexuality of the partners simply doesn't matter.

If you're a WOMAN now, the same applies. If you feel nicely feminine, you've probably just joined the Virgo class. If you recognize the genuine Virgoan asexuality within you, you may well have been born under Virgo quite a few times – or your Key Life could be straight out of the monastic Middle Ages.

What kind of Life?

There are four main kinds of life that you could be leading.

It could be a LIFE OF CONTINUITY if you feel comfortably Virgoan: thoroughly true to the sign's characteristics, but not extremely so. You will have several distinct Virgoan skills: clever with numbers, dextrous at handicrafts, neat and tidy in your habits. You may recognize your limitations, but know that you're doing a good job.

A LIFE OF REACTION means that you've entered the Virgoan consciousness briefly for a particular purpose: usually to get your own back on someone who inflicted frigidity on you in the past. If you feel driven by an inner obsession, you could be a 'reactor'. Equally, if you feel horribly guilty about not being Virgoan enough, then you may be getting a short, sharp lesson in the need for tidiness and decency.

Some Virgoans are definitely in the midst of a DEAD-END life, when they find themselves driven into a cul-de-sac of fussy, cold antagonism. A series of crises in their lives should force them to turn their back on heartless puritanism, and start being warm again. But this may not happen until their next life, of course.

Finally, quite a few souls enjoy a SECOND-BREATH LIFE under Virgo. Symbolically it can be asserted that Virgo is the start of the spiritual Zodiac, when new-born souls, fresh out of heaven, begin the slow descent into materialism. After some hairy experiences elsewhere in the Zodiac, you could be starting anew in Virgo – especially if you feel full of New Year resolutions all through your life!

Spirit in Libra: Sun 180 – 209

Your Character in this Life

Your Libran spirit resembles a pair of scales: forever in search of the point of equilibrium. Or it's like the still centre of the whirlwind, free from the buffets of the rough, tough world outside.

You are constantly looking for peace and harmony. You thrive on friendship and etiquette, the small change of polite society. If you spot conflict, you shy away from it. If you see dirt, you hastily sweep it under the carpet. You have a fatal attraction for the *appearance* of life; you do not greatly care for the structure underneath.

Sadly for Librans, reality intrudes. When crisis threatens, you cannot easily cope. You are nonplussed by choice. You hate reaching a firm decision on anything, for to pick one alternative is to reject the other – and rejection is anathema to a Libran.

At your best, you are the soul of kindness. Central to your life is the need to be successful in human relationships. Without friendship you feel bereft, incomplete, without a purpose in life. But within an aura of affection, especially one created by a happy marriage, you flower as a personality.

Your Overall Development

There are several stages of Zodiacal development stretched over many lifetimes. You must decide for yourself what level you have reached.

The PRIMITIVE Libran is a hopeless creature, totally dependent on others for strength, love and direction in life. He puts all his faith in his loved one, and feels desolate if he is then abandoned. He is a dabbler at everything and expert in none. He puts off all decisions until *mañana*. He is soft and weak.

The AVERAGE Libran is trying to be more self-sufficient, though he is certainly not suited to a life of solitude. He is quite gifted in the arts, and can create an atmosphere of charm and relaxation wherever he goes. He knows that he tends to be too lazy for his own good. If he's lucky, he meets his soul-mate – and the ensuing marriage is as sweet and loving as any could be.

Metaphorically the Libran must move from lazy-bones to willing helper, from 'little woman' to genuine partner.

The ADVANCED Libran is much more positive in his approach to life. He actively brings people together in peace and friendship. In his personal dealings he has great tact, but he's not afraid to take his courage in both hands and speak bluntly, if need be. He praises rather than blames, and is adept at reaching sensible compromises.

Careers that you may have followed in the past will have been those dealing with people rather than products. You may have been talented in designing fashion, painting, furniture-making, etc, or spent time in the theatre. You could also have been trained in the diplomatic world, journalism or advertising.

Spiritually there are strong links with Buddhism, so you have almost certainly spent many lives in the Far East. But equally your Libran spirit will have been shaped by many humble lives as housewife, consort, geisha, toady or king's favourite!

Your Sexual History

Libra is pre-eminently the female, *yin*-oriented spirit. It is expressed most effectively by a thoroughly feminine soul. At the same time, it can probably be checked and balanced and made tougher by being embodied by a man.

If you're a MAN now, the likelihood is that you have recently been a woman – or will change sex in your next life. If you are leading quite a few lives in Libra, you could be a man in just this one before reverting to womanhood again.

If you're a WOMAN now, you are probably in the midst of a sustained bout of Libran development – mainly as a woman. Alternatively, it's quite common for a man to spend a single life of reaction as a woman – just to see what it's like.

What kind of Life?

There are four main kinds of life that you could be leading.

If you're involved in a LIFE OF CONTINUITY, you feel thoroughly at home in the Libran psyche. You're probably female, skilled in the arts, and popular with many kinds of people. Within your Libran spirit you should feel quite grown-up and capable.

If, on the other hand, you're leading a LIFE OF REACTION, you will pay exaggerated importance to the relationships around you. There could be a fated quality about your marriage(s), as though you're drawn ineluctably towards your partners, whether you like them or not.

In such a life, you will feel trapped by your own indecisiveness. In general, you will experience the helplessness of the Libran spirit when confronted by other, more dominant souls.

A DEAD-END LIFE occurs relatively rarely within the Libran sphere of influence – for the whole point of this Zodiac sign is the avoidance of extremes. A Libran dead-end life resembles a life of reaction, except that you feel that the failure of your life is entirely your own fault, instead of being caused by others.

You feel that your Libran spirit has nothing more to offer – and in consequence you want to turn your back on your whole nature and somehow start again.

Finally, a SECOND-BREATH LIFE is quite a likely occurrence under Libra. It's a lovely sign to return to, after a long sojourn in the heavier, *yang*-infested regions of the Zodiac.

Spirit in Scorpio: Sun 210 – 239

Your Character in this Life

Your Scorpio spirit is like a mountain lake: still, chilly, reflective, held in by gaunt shores. It has a huge amount of force, waiting to be released. It also has murky inner depths that can't be seen from outside!

You take life seriously; you cannot treat it as a light-hearted affair. Instead, you concentrate fiercely on the battles and passions and hoped-for victories. You take the whole human condition seriously, but most of all you are serious about yourself: who you are, what you are doing here, where you are going when you die. (More people from Scorpio will read this book than from any other Sun-sign!)

You like being mysterious, keeping other people guessing, hiding your secrets away from the common gaze but delighting in probing into other people's secrets.

At times you can seem your own worst enemy, either because you pursue a hopeless – or wrongheaded – cause, or because you refuse to compromise and accept defeat. You are obsessive in searching for the one career, partner, mission or destiny that will give meaning to your life. You can be a true fanatic!

Your Overall Development

There are several stages of Zodiacal development stretched

over many lifetimes. You must decide for yourself what level you have reached.

The PRIMITIVE Scorpian is a defensive creature with a poisonous sting when he feels threatened. Often he has a chip on his shoulder. When he takes a fancy to someone, he becomes enormously possessive – and jealous if slighted. His task is to try to tame the fierce, vengeful passions raging in his breast.

The AVERAGE Scorpian has plenty of emotional power, but he is learning to direct it into worthwhile aims. He is excellent in dangerous situations, keeping his nerve and encouraging others to do likewise. He is a great self-improver, but can be too critical of himself at times.

He is moving, in a manner of speaking, from outlaw to sheriff, witch-doctor to psychiatrist, criminal to hero. There is a greater range of temperament within the Scorpian spirit than elsewhere in the Zodiac.

The ADVANCED Scorpian has exceptional qualities of courage in the face of adversity. He is prepared to make sacrifices in a noble cause, and can inspire others to heights of determined resistance. Even in peaceful surroundings, he seems to test himself to the utmost. Nothing is too much trouble.

Careers that you may have followed in the past are anything calling for single-minded dedication. You will have enjoyed being tested to the limits of your capacity. This will have included being a soldier or, more probably, a sailor, perhaps a doctor or surgeon, a lawyer, or worker in heavy industrial conditions.

Spiritually there are links with Islam and Judaism, and also, long ago, with voodoo, black magic and similar cults. Perhaps not so long ago, either! But equally your Scorpian spirit will have been shaped by tough, manly conditions in the armed services, or by womanly courage holding a family together through hard times.

Your Sexual History
Scorpio is meant to be a feminine Zodiac sign, but its strength and will-power would normally be linked with soul development in a male body.

If you're a MAN now, however, there's no guarantee that you were a man in your previous life. Since Scorpio is, pre-eminently, the sign of reaction, you could easily have temporarily assumed a male personality to pay someone back for past misdeeds. Remember, Scorpio can be a terribly *sadistic* spirit – and it's tempting, as a man, to dominate other people, women especially, in a way that is bound to create hurtful future karma for yourself. Your task is to control your emotional power, not give way to it.

The same applies, obviously, if you're a WOMAN in this life – especially if you're an introverted Scorpian feeling hard done by. You could have been a man previously, now learning the hard way how bitter it is to be lonely. But it's wrong to think of your Scorpian spirit as always depressing. As a woman in particular, you may well discover your true love in this life. Glorious emotional discoveries and surprises can occur under the Scorpio banner!

What kind of Life?
There are four main kinds of life that you could be leading.

A LIFE OF CONTINUITY is certainly possible under Scorpio. If you are leading this sort of life, you will have definite Scorpio skills (as manager, healer or self-reliant man of action) and will feel fairly at home within the Scorpian spirit. You will feel strongly that there's a special destiny or mission awaiting you in this life.

Many Scorpians are leading LIVES OF REACTION. You've been plunged into the Scorpio temperament to work out karma that's accumulated from the past. There may be one particular difficulty (especially a worrisome marriage) that needs to be lived through. If you feel that you're sometimes your own worst enemy, and if you get paranoid about one special person, or if you have a deep-seated phobia that won't go away – then you're leading a life of reaction.

Equally common, I'm afraid, is the Scorpionic DEAD-END LIFE! In fact, there are more dead-enders born between October 23rd and November 23rd than at any other time of year! It is the ideal temperament for ferociously digging an ever-deeper pit...until you can't get out. If, as is quite possible under Scorpio, you feel suicidal, depressed, without hope or ambition, you are maybe leading this kind of life. But remember, there's always a way out!

SECOND-BREATH LIVES do not happen under the auspices of Scorpio. Quite simply, they are mutually exclusive, and it's a contradiction in terms to *think* of a second-breath Scorpio life!

Spirit in Sagittarius: Sun 240 – 269

Your Character in this Life
Your Sagittarian spirit is like a forest fire: ardent, adventurous, blown this way and that, and dangerously attractive!

You have a breezy, buccaneering quality about you. You love to turn things inside out, keeping other people on their toes. In arguments, which you love, you throw in new ideas like rubber-balls, just to see which way they bounce. You are the kite-flyer, the trail-blazer, the kind of person who loves having a go.

You long to see round the next corner or over the brow of the distant horizon. Your inquisitiveness is endless; you love to ask why, and with this knowledge you gradually assemble a world-view that is broad-minded, full of vision and, hopefully, tolerant.

In temperament, you are cheerful, but you can lack stamina and concentration, forever taking up a new career or hobby and casually dropping it after a while. For you need independence. As soon as you start feeling trapped, you head for the hills!

Your Overall Development

There are several stages of Zodiacal development stretched over many lifetimes. You must decide for yourself what level you have reached.

The PRIMITIVE Sagittarian is wild, cheeky and tactless. He does what he likes, achieves little, and prides himself on his freedom – freedom without responsibility.

The AVERAGE Sagittarian accepts that some discipline is needed. He has a built-in sense of decency and fair play, and will defend other people from attack; but he still has difficulty in seeing a job through to the bitter end. He tends to be a bit of a preacher or barrack-room lawyer, laying down the law and certain that he's right.

His psychological journey is from dare-devil to sportsman, cowboy to entrepreneur.

The ADVANCED Sagittarian is a warm and noble individual, following his own conscience, beholden to nobody, and having a generous-hearted outlook on life. He has a keen intellect, especially in science, but also likes to play a role in public affairs, helping to establish broad associations, international groups and so forth.

Careers that you may have followed in the past are anything calling for personal initiative, variety and enthusiasm – from engineer, prospector, lawyer, journalist and writer to teacher and publisher.

Spiritually there are links with the Unitarian and Methodist movements as well as the Socratic schools in Ancient Greece. Any intellectual activity that encouraged a questioning approach is a possible training-ground for the Sagittarian spirit.

Your Sexual History

Sagittarius is mainly a *yang*-oriented Zodiac sign. The spirit of enterprise and freedom which it develops is a male characteristic, and Sagittarian women often have a tomboyish attitude to life.

If you're a MAN now, you could be in a life of continuity – or a second-breath life. It depends on your attitude. If you're a muscular, open-air sort of Sagittarian, you've been a man for quite a number of lives. If you're a softer, amiable sort of fellow, you may well just have changed from being a woman.

If you're a WOMAN now, you were probably a man in your earlier life. You are more pushy than many other women, able to stand on your feet, and keen to tackle new projects. The women's movement of the past few years suits you admirably, except that you have nothing against men: you simply like to be in charge of yourself.

What kind of Life?

There are four main kinds of life that you could be leading.

A LIFE OF CONTINUITY is quite frequent among Sagittarians. You are leading this kind of life if you are athletic, outward-bound, full of enthusiasm and yet aware of your moral responsibilities. You may have a distinct ability with spoken and written words. If you have an overpowering interest in natural history or one of the sciences, this is certainly a continuing interest from past lives.

You'll be leading a LIFE OF REACTION if you have a strong inner desire to preach for – or against – a particular issue, or if you have an adversary whom you want to criticize. In each case, you are fighting back against views – or people – with whom you've differed in the past.

If you play fast and loose with a sweetheart, you may simply be reversing the relationship from an earlier life.

DEAD-END LIVES are not frequently encountered among Sagittarian souls, if only because the Sagittarian spirit can always find an escape route out of difficulties! But if you feel you are impossibly restless and unreliable, if you long to change your ways and settle down, then it's possible you have reached the dead-end of the Sagittarian experience.

There are many SECOND-BREATH LIVES led by Sagittarians today. It can be a wonderfully liberating experience – the chance to breathe again after many stifling problems in an earlier life.

Spirit in Capricorn: Sun 270 – 299

Your Character in this Life

Your Capricorn spirit is like the winter landscape: sometimes frosty and unyielding, but preserving its strength in case things get even worse!

You are motivated by the will to survive – to cope with life. However difficult the path ahead, you will travel it – even though you must close in on yourself, become self-contained and solitary until the perilous journey is over.

So you can be stony in your temperament, giving little away that is unnecessary, concentrating with great patience on the essential tasks in hand. This control over your life – which means over yourself and, by extension, the whole community – is central to the Capricorn outlook. But it is your goal rather than starting-point; and as a young person you may have felt fearfully shy and inadequate. Capricorn people often don't get going until their thirties.

Ambition and defensiveness are the two sides of the Capricorn aim in life. You seem to have a wall around you from the moment of birth – a wall to hide behind, if need be, or clamber up to be king of the castle, if you so desire. In just the same way, subservience and snobbery go hand in hand – and the combination can lead to hypocrisy, of course.

Your Overall Development

There are several stages of Zodiacal development stretched over many lifetimes. You must decide for yourself what level you have reached.

The PRIMITIVE Capricornian is immersed in material attitudes – so much so that he doesn't recognize ideals, kindness or generosity as virtues at all. He makes the mistake of always obeying the letter – never the spirit – of the law.

The AVERAGE Capricornian is learning to be bolder – and more mellow – than he wants to be. He is good at management, engineering, science and detailed work of all kinds. In his ambitious mood, he can still treat other people as mere rungs in his own ladder of advancement, but with his developed sense of guilt he now knows that when he's in his 'efficient' mood he does act heartlessly towards people who don't fit into his scheme of things.

In a manner of speaking, he is moving from Scrooge to Father Christmas. He is learning how to be fair and responsible at the same time.

Finally, the ADVANCED Capricornian has a wonderful reliability and trustworthiness. He has a deep sense of moral justice. He does not like the past for its own sake, but because he cannot bear to throw anything away, however old-fashioned it may be. He is a real pragmatist, and will abandon a treasured principle or theory once it has been shown not to work in practice.

Careers that you may have followed in the past will have developed your organizational skills, also your brain-power and money-handling ability. You could have been a banker, teacher, trader, ore extractor or bureaucrat.

Spiritually there are links with the Puritan movement but also with the Catholic hierarchy. You could well have been part of an ascetic community one life, and a Vatican bigwig the next.

Your Sexual History

Capricorn is not a strongly sexual Zodiac sign. It tends to repress the instincts and deny a free flow of pleasure. Both men and women are capable of embodying this temperament, though it seems to suit the male personality better.

If you're a MAN now, you have probably been this sex for several lives – especially if you feel slightly antipathetic to women. There is a danger of becoming a misogynist if you stay under the male Capricorn banner for too long, treating women as sex objects or possessions instead of as equal human beings.

If you're a WOMAN now, you may have been a free-and-easy man before, returning now to learn what it's like to be lonely and introvert. Equally, you could come back as a woman, after a series of capable lives as men, in order to be an effective pioneer businesswoman or stateswoman in the unisex 20th century.

What kind of Life?

There are four main kinds of life that you could be leading.

A LIFE OF CONTINUITY means that you have been developing your Capricorn spirit over a series of lives. You can recognize yourself here if you feel thoroughly at home in the Capricorn temperament, have definite skills as a manager and organizer, have a developed sense of guilt and morality, and feel strongly that you should play an important part in the running of the community around you.

A LIFE OF REACTION is equally common under Capricorn. This means that you have returned, for one life only, to learn at first hand how hurtful the puritan spirit can be. You could have played fast and loose with people before; now you are expressing the same bleakness you imposed on them. Or you have been dominated by harsh, unyielding people – and now you have the chance – if you wish to take it – of being similarly harsh in return.

A DEAD-END LIFE is very likely under Capricorn. If the purpose of life is to descend into matter and then struggle free of it, Capricorn represents the nadir of this two-way journey. Indeed, the point of return *must* take place during a Capricornian incarnation.

Finally, a SECOND-BREATH LIFE is highly unlikely as part of the Capricorn experience. It simply isn't a jolly enough temperament.

Spirit in Aquarius: Sun 300 – 329

Your Character in this Life
Your Aquarian spirit is like a snowscape: crisp, unreal, transforming something familiar into a crystalline new vision.

In much the same way, you have the capacity to see life from an unusual standpoint, spotting things that the rest of us might not notice, presenting ideas in a novel way to make them more interesting and lively.

Your primary motivation is the pursuit of truth. This may be the objective truth of science or, more probably, the subjective truth of the social reformer, moral do-gooder or political crusader. Facts allied to altruism is the typical Aquarian mix; you are interested in tomorrow rather than yesterday; you believe in progress; and above all you believe in mankind's power to surmount the difficulties of the environment. *Mind over Matter* is your motto.

You like to assert mental mastery over your own turbulent emotional nature. Aquarians give this cool, calm and collected image. You seem unshockable – and whatever your task in hand, there's a voice of reason telling you the right course of action to follow. In one sense, you're like a computer: affable, observant, inquiring, dispassionate . . . and bloodless!

Your Overall Development
There are several stages of Zodiacal development stretched over many lifetimes. You must decide for yourself what level you have reached.

The PRIMITIVE Aquarian is a complete nonconformist – unpredictable, always going his own way, never really 'belonging' to a marriage, family or working group. He can be tactless in blurting out the truth, insensitive to other people's moods, and too theoretical and indecisive when prompt action is needed.

The AVERAGE Aquarian is putting ideals into action in his everyday life. He is learning the hard lesson – for him – of showing warmth and passion in close encounters with other human beings! But mainly he's learning how to work in groups, co-operating with others, developing a group approach to work and leisure.

In effect, through evolution he's moving from iconoclast to individual, spectator to participator.

The ADVANCED Aquarian is a wonderfully inventive and resourceful type. He can create a happy atmosphere where everyone is treated as an equal, for Aquarians are notoriously unsnobbish and go out of their way to treat everyone fairly. He may be a prophet of the future, or he may unearth ancient wisdom and present it in a fresh idiom that everyone can understand.

Careers that you may have followed in the past could be anything that tests the brain and encourages ingenuity. These could have been early forms of social work, land management, academic research, health care (especially the mentally ill) and simply as a traveller.

Spiritually there are important links with occult groups throughout history: the masons, rosicrucians, gnostics, kabbalists – any association, in short, that has been linked with the ancient wisdom. There is also a powerful association with ancient Greece.

Your Sexual History

Aquarius is another neutral Zodiac sign. Like Gemini and, to a lesser extent, Virgo, Aquarius is really asexual, wanting to forget about gender differences rather than accentuate them.

Certainly, in this century, all Aquarians are learning the essential *humanity* of people, instead of dividing them into separate sexual groups. To this extent, you are in the vanguard of progress.

If you're a MAN now, you could have been either sex in the past. If you feel the differences in the sexes is vitally important, you are probably having a life of reaction – or just starting a long series of lives of continuity.

If you're a WOMAN now, you are learning to place your womanly instincts to one side, and give top priority to idealistic and human attitudes. This could be a life of reaction after an over-abundance of emotion in a previous life. The sex that you were in this previous life is not desperately important.

What kind of Life?
There are four main kinds of life that you could be leading.

A LIFE OF CONTINUITY means that you've been an Aquarian for some lives now. If so, you'll be a cool customer indeed, good at mathematics, well able to keep your feelings under control, full of ideals for the future.

A LIFE OF REACTION is relatively uncommon under Aquarius. In a way, Aquarius is like the proverbial bucket of water thrown over coupling dogs: useful as a quick antidote to too much emotionality in the past. If you have been an extremist of any persuasion in the past, Aquarius is good for inculcating reason and moderation.

A DEAD-END LIFE is rare under Aquarius – certainly at the moment, when it's the one Zodiac sign whose possibilities stretch endlessly into the new Aquarian Age.

However, many Aquarians at the moment are enjoying SECOND-BREATH LIVES. After the pain and humiliation of the past, it's a relief for them to enjoy the relative freedom and open-mindedness of the Aquarian outlook on life.

Spirit in Pisces: Sun 330 – 359

Your Character in this Life
Your Pisces spirit is like the ocean: eternally moving, never

going anywhere, alert to the slightest nuance of wind or current.

In just the same way, you can easily adapt yourself to fit into the prevailing mood; but you lack that strong motivating drive that impels people to the top.

Quite literally, at times, you are an absent-minded person, for you do not live in your mentality very much, far more in your feelings and intuitions. There's an easy flow between your spirit and psyche, and ideas and moods and apprehensions bubble up from the depths without obvious reason. You work in a fluid way, without hard edges. You cannot always explain your beliefs, and are therefore close to a mystical attitude.

Your great gift is kindness. Like the water which is your symbol, you can flow into other people's hearts, sympathizing and pouring compassion out. You can identify so readily because you lack a strong sense of personal identity in the first place.

Inevitably you find it hard to concentrate and persevere in a particular direction. You want to be free from restrictions – free to be moved this way and that by any passing pressure.

Your Overall Development
There are several stages of Zodiacal development stretched over many lifetimes. You must decide for yourself what level you have reached.

The PRIMITIVE Piscean is just a wet fish – droopy, a victim of his own moods and inner fears, over-emotional with no self-control at all. He is devious, always trying to slip away from responsibilities, doing anything to avoid a definite commitment.

The AVERAGE Piscean needs a happy, creative environment in which to operate. Contentment is more important than achievement. He must guard against helping people so much that he never helps himself. He is learning to balance his escapist urges with his desire for emotional security. And best of all, he is learning how to turn his inner dreams and visions into practical use in the everyday world.

Metaphorically, he is developing from an innocent to an artist, from victim to victor.

Finally, the ADVANCED Piscean is strong but sensitive, able to withstand life's buffets without being blown off-course. He has a heart full of charity, and can teach humanity how to feel simply yet deeply about life.

Spiritually there are links with medieval Christianity, and also, much further back, with Druidism and nature worship.

Your Sexual History

Pisces is mainly a *yin*-oriented, female Zodiac sign. It encourages the growth of sensitivity, making you want to protect and help people in distress.

If you're a MAN now, you have either just changed sex – or are just about to. Pisces is the ideal melting pot of emotions, where the male temperament can most easily identify with female attitudes, and vice versa. Certainly you're unlikely to have had many – or any – male Piscean lives in a row.

But you might well have had a series of lives as a man elsewhere in the Zodiac, and are just having one dip in the Piscean bath, softening you up for a new series of lives as a woman.

If you're a WOMAN now, you may well have had a series of lives in this Zodiac sign. Pisces is one of the gentlest of all signs for womanhood, and many valuable lessons in the use – and abuse – of love can be gained here.

You could certainly have just changed sex from an earlier male incarnation, but it's unlikely that you'll become a man in your next life.

What kind of Life?

There are four main kinds of life that you could be leading.

A LIFE OF CONTINUITY means that you are developing your Piscean spirit over a series of lives. This is comparatively unlikely at the present stage of the world, though it may well have been true in the past. Few souls have the opportunity in our bustling modern world to be a poet in an ivory tower, life after life.

A LIFE OF REACTION is very frequent under Pisces. If you have been needlessly cruel in a previous life, it's natural for the tables to be turned, so that you can play victim for a while.

This applies, too, if you have earlier forced people into a uncongenial lifestyle, or bullied them, or ignored their finer feelings.

A DEAD-END LIFE is certainly possible under Pisces. If you are totally escapist, especially if you become an alcoholic or drug addict, you could have reached a cul-de-sac in your Piscean experience.

CHAPTER EIGHT

Psyche

In Chapter Six, FIGURING IT OUT, you were shown how to calculate the position of the Moon. This, very broadly, establishes the nature of your psyche: the kind of inner consciousness you possess in this life.

There are twelve different kinds of psyche, represented by the various signs of the Zodiac. In this chapter you can look up the section referring to your psyche, according to your Moon number, and learn something about your inner nature. Treat everything you read as poetry rather than exact fact. My remarks are meant to inspire your own intuition, triggering memories buried deep within you.

Psyche in Aries: Moon 0 – 29

Your Emotional Nature

Whatever your outer manner may be, your inner emotional nature is brisk and volatile. You have a lively response to events. Whenever something, however trivial, occurs, you have an instant reaction, be it anger or enthusiasm or merriment. You aren't slow to speak your mind, nor are you frightened of the consequences of doing so.

In short, you have a robust emotional nature, erring on the side of brashness rather than sensibility. Your whole instinct is to take action – to intervene, not stand on the sidelines. This means you can certainly be over-hasty at times, making tactless remarks perhaps or losing your temper when you should really have kept your cool. But it's wrong to suggest that you have a moody disposition. You don't feel revenge or irritation for long. Once you have let off steam, you feel calm and refreshed, even though the people around you may still be stunned by the strength of your emotions.

All in all, this is a male-oriented, action-packed sort of inner disposition – hard-headed, coping with clashes, keen to come to terms with reality. Not so much a stream of consciousness, more like a torrent!

Your Folk Memory

Certainly, with Moon in this part of the sky, you are firmly locked into the physical world, but this doesn't mean that you have no contact at all with psychic life. On the contrary, you may well have some vivid dreams, for this is the only time, when you are relaxed in sleep, that your unconscious mind can reach you.

The part of our Folk Memory that attracts you is the battle for survival. This summons up your adrenalin, restoring your vigour and determination. Favourite dreams could well centre around the conquering hero, either slaying the dragon or returning in triumph to welcoming crowds. Sometimes you'll be the hero yourself, sometimes one of his adoring fans; this will depend on whether you are feeling confident or anxious about events in your everyday life. If the hero is being brave on his own, you are trying to draw fresh lungfuls of willpower. If the hero is helping others – rescuing them from a burning house, for instance – you are really pleading for co-operation, asking your Unconscious to get other people to be more amenable in everyday life!

You mustn't think that all your dreams are based on aggressiveness. Other typical dreams will involve sport or engineering feats such as building bridges. If you dream of our Folk experience, you could be taking part in some great migration, or hunting for food, or defending other people from a sudden catastrophe.

Links with the Past

Clearly you have been evolving along a masterful path of development in the recent past. You have been learning how to be strong and effortful, swift and decisive, like a hunter in search of food. This doesn't mean that you have necessarily learnt your lesson well, but at least some of these qualities have been incorporated into your psyche.

How, where and when? It's likely that people with Moon in Aries have returned relatively quickly to Earth. What's more, they may easily have been caught up in a tempestuous situation in their last life which roused powerful and unresolved emotions. In addition, they were probably, though not exclusively, male. Put all these factors together and it's likely that many young Moon-in-Aries people alive today were among the millions of soldiers who died in the First World War.

Certainly there will have been some competitive element in your recent life, probably among a group of males. Besides a military experience, this could have been a hostile home environment (with rivalry between brothers) or an ambitious working life where, to succeed, you had to be ruthless towards the opposition.

This life could well have been spent in England or Germany, or under the colonial rule of one of these nations. But your independent outlook could equally have been gained as an emigrant to a strange country – a settler driving westwards over America or a convict transported to Australia.

There's a rough, blunt edge to your emotional nature that suggests a lot of unfinished karma: fierce quarrels to be resolved, tense inner knots yet to be gently untied. So your background was probably hard, without much mothering. You led an open-air self-sufficient lifestyle. As a result, you may lack some style and polish now.

I would expect you to enjoy stories about King Arthur, operas by Wagner, historical novels set in pioneer country and be drawn (happily) to Elizabethan England and (less happily) to Prussian Germany.

Links with Sun-Signs

With your Moon-in-Aries nature you are an individualist, which is admirable in some ways but awkward at times when mixing and co-operating with others. Here's your brief guide to the way you relate to various Sun-signs – including yourself! Also included is a Moon-in-Aries celebrity born under each Sun-sign, which may help you to see how spirit and psyche combine in an individual.

Sun-Sign	Your own character	Relating to Others
Aries	Fiery, self-willed, highly independent. Your air of command comes straight from experience in another life. Example: MARLON BRANDO.	Fine links with Aries people, but you aren't very tolerant of each other. Likely sex link in earlier life together.
Taurus	Stolid on the surface, but tempestuous underneath. A cowboy trying to be a farmer! Example: actor GEORGE COLE.	Very different people, aren't you? Could well have been enemies in the past. You are the trouble-maker, usually!
Gemini	Logical, young at mind, impatient at others. You were an intelligent, active person in an earlier life. Example: TV commentator FRED DINENAGE.	Good mixture – lively and vivacious, quarrelsome but able to cope with each other. Probably male friends in a previous incarnation.

Sun-Sign Your own character	Relating to Others
Cancer Stormy and emotional, vain but shy! Maybe you've changed sex since your last life. Inner peace is your great aim. Example: NATALIE WOOD.	You will dominate this relationship at first, but a Cancer person will gradually exert influence over you.
Leo Warm-hearted individual, but at times you're too hot to handle! Almost certainly a glamorous and commanding figure in earlier life. Example: JACKIE ONASSIS.	Good links, fine for a love affair but a bit too lively for a long-term relationship. Lots of chemistry, not much commonsense.
Virgo Clash here between spirit and psyche: a hard-headed idealist. Probably developed a special talent in previous lives. Example: LEONARD BERNSTEIN.	Can be many nagging little quarrels. Better for business relationship than marriage.
Libra Nice mixture of strength and charm. May have male and female qualities equally mixed. Can be a lack of direction in life. Example: MARC BOLAN.	You have the upper hand, and can be insensitive at times. Good for a marriage, provided Libra is also assertive.
Scorpio Tough, sardonic, wanting to achieve plenty. May have deep hang-ups	Battle of wills! Be prepared for Scorpio's moody silences! You keep the

Sun-Sign   Your own Character   Relating to Others

over power, and may have acted badly in past life. Example: JOHN CLEESE.

relationship on move, Scorpio keeps it together.

Sagittarius Spirit and psyche in smooth harmony. You radiate warmth and appeal, and were a free-thinking, independent person in previous life. Example: NATASHA PARRY.

Wonderful for free-as-air relationship, without heavy responsibilities. Be careful you don't go your own ways.

Capricorn Powerful character full of determination. Logical and principled. You will have exercised considerable authority in a previous life. Example: SIMONE DE BEAUVOIR.

You get tired of Capricorn's caution, but you can tackle a job of work together with discipline and speed. Obviously you have worked together in the past.

Aquarius A spritely character, full of surprises. You combine energy with enterprise, and have probably a special task to do in this life. Example: BARRY HUMPHREYS.

Excellent mixture, because you both love your freedom. May well have been colleagues in a previous life together.

Pisces There's a deep split in your personality, with an aggressive streak coming to terms with

You may bully poor Pisces, but actually you have much to learn from each other. Almost certainly some

Sun-Sign   Your own Character   Relating to Others

great idealism and
creativity. Example:
A Clockwork Orange author
ANTHONY BURGESS.

quality of karmic revenge in
your relationship.

Psyche in Taurus: Moon 30 – 59

Your Emotional Nature

You have a deep, rich inner nature, rooted in the instincts.
Your response to life is rarely hurried. You take your time,
consulting your own gut reactions, weighing the consequences, often following tradition and preferring to stick to a
well-worn path instead of branching out on your own.

In your emotional disposition you have good earthy likes and
dislikes: food and drink, bodily comforts and warm, familiar
friendships are what you appreciate, which means that you're
drawn to a loving family circle. Your sense of possessiveness is
strongly marked. What you own, you love; and what you love,
you strive hard to own.

Inevitably you can seem stubborn, even greedy at times, but
generally you should be popular company. With the Moon in
this position, your inner emotional demeanour is like well-
rotted compost – the result of a long, patient development in
the past and now an admirably fertile instrument for growth in
the future.

Your Folk Memory

Although you are rooted in physical reality, you have some
fine instinctual links with your Unconscious. Many of your
everyday emotions, based, you may think, on commonsense,
stem really from the Unconscious, even though you may not
realize it! Indeed, in lots of ways you are a living embodiment
of the Folk Memory, always responding to life in the same way
as Stone Age man would have done!

You are capable, in your dreams, of reverberating back through history, hearing the murmurs, so to speak, of ancestral voices, identifying yourself with their attitudes. You have a wonderful sense of place, and a favourite dream for Moon-in-Taurus people involves a much-loved homestead in the countryside where you, together with your large family, live in halcyon rural bliss.

A typical nightmare, on the other hand, could involve a fear of suffocation, with you trapped in a pot-hole or city subway or a room where the four walls are relentlessly moving towards you. Here you would be warned by your Unconscious that your Moon-in-Taurus psyche is smothering other qualities in your personality. The reverse is also true; if you dream of suffering from vertigo – the fear of heights – your Taurean psyche is prompting you to seek more security in your everyday life. Don't always follow this advice. Be more adventurous than you want to be, for your Taurean psyche is a peasant at heart, frightened of leaving familiar surroundings. And in your personal Dramarathon your soul cannot get stuck in a rut for long.

Links with the Past

Your whole instinct is towards settling down, making the best of circumstances, following the habits of a lifetime or – if you believe in reincarnation – many lifetimes.

So your recent past life or two have been spent concentrating on earthly matters, immersing yourself in a steady routine and perhaps identifying yourself with the rhythms of the seasons. You could have lived on the land, farming food from the soil, or you could have been a city farmer, sowing seeds of invest-ment that would grow into a harvest of dividends.

In the past two centuries, people have increasingly moved from the countryside into the cities. If you feel that your Taurean psyche is the source of your money-making skills, you may well have reincarnated fairly quickly from a 19th-century businessman, perhaps. But if you feel that your present-day psyche puts you in touch with life on the farm, it may well be a throwback to a series of lives spent close to the soil.

This could have been almost anywhere in the world, for Taurus is not a strongly nationalistic Zodiac sign. It has some link with Mother Russia, however, so if you have a sentimental fondness for the rolling steppes you may well have been one of the toiling pre-Revolutionary peasants.

Certainly I'd expect you to have a strong sense of 'I've been here before' at times. Your attachment to places is so deep that you would probably recognize any home that you'd occupied in a previous life.

Moon in Taurus suggests a history of togetherness. Through many lives you will have learnt how to be self-sufficient and co-operative at the same time.

Links with Spirit
On the whole you're a good mixer, especially among your nearest and dearest or when entertaining friends in your own home. But you can be wary of strangers at first – all part of your 'peasant' awareness of life! Here's your sign-by-sign guide to the way your own spirit and psyche combine, and also how you relate to other spirits. Also you'll find a Moon-in-Taurus celebrity born under each Sun-sign, which should show how spirit and psyche combine in an individual.

Sun-Sign Your own Character	*Relating to Others*
Aries Outwardly you seem very lively and go-ahead, but inwardly you are much more quiet and settled. Example: singer DIANA ROSS.	There's a definite clash between you. You'll find Aries too boisterous and indiscreet while Aries thinks you are dull and stolid at times.

Sun-Sign   Your own Character   Relating to Others

Taurus A highly determined and stable individual, though people find you too stubborn at times. Example: KING HUSSEIN OF JORDAN.

Obviously you have fine links with Taurean people. This is a wonderful combination for husband and wife: warm, deep links.

Gemini Your feelings are warm and sensual, but highly restless. In this life you are really letting go. Example: JOAN COLLINS.

Sometimes you'll find it hard to keep up with Gemini folk. They are on a livelier ego-trip in this life than you are.

Cancer A family type, marvellous at making others feel at home. Probably leading a continuity life. Example: guitarist JULIAN BREAM.

Excellent combination. You marry together well. Could well have been in the same family in previous lives.

Leo Highly creative, sensual, obstinate! This life seems a holiday after previous hard-working lives. Example: MICK JAGGER.

You are more workaday and sensible than Leo. Many rows due to pride. Could have been rivals in previous lives.

Virgo Caught between ideals and expediency. Can be dry as dust. Possibly coming to a dead-end in this life. Example: actor NICOL WILLIAMSON.

Good if matter-of-fact links here. You may have worked together in the past, perhaps in medicine, business or education.

Libra Sweet-natured and loving, the result of much

Wonderful ability to like and love each other. You

affection in earlier lives. You probably have artistic taste developed in the past. Example: ANGIE DICKINSON.

will try to dominate the relationship. Good links for marriage partners and sweethearts.

Scorpio There's a conflict between your higher and lower selves. At one level you like comfort; at another, you want to turn life upside down. Example: PETER COOK.

A fiercely proud relationship. You will find Scorpio too prickly and jealous; while you are considered too cosy at times.

Sagittarius In earlier lives you developed a sound practical base from which to be adventurous. Definitely a life to break free from the past. Example: CHRISTOPHER PLUMMER.

You distrust each other, but can learn so much by mixing together! You find Sagittarius too restless. Could have been distant friends in a number of earlier lives.

Capricorn A heavy personality, probably carrying a load of karma from the past. You are fixed in a pattern, and need to break free. Example: GEORGE FOREMAN.

Good businesslike links, but inclined to be too cool and inhuman at times. There could be plenty of deep-seated anger – and boredom – between you.

Aquarius Interesting combination of down-to-earth commonsense and high altruism. A 'second-

You admire the free-wheeling spirit of Aquarius, but cannot match it. Once again, you can provide the

Sun-Sign   Your own Character   *Relating to Others*

breath' personality, building on past achievements. Example: GERMAINE GREER.

comfort to Aquarius that you gave in the past.

Pisces Tricky mixture: very creative but emotionally unstable. A firm grip on reality is constantly being weakened. Example: film-maker PIER PAOLO PASOLINI.

At a soul level there can be many links, but in everyday terms there can be misunderstandings.

Psyche in Gemini: Moon 60 – 89

Your Emotional Nature

Inwardly you're a lively creature, veering from one mood to another. You do things at speed, reach hasty decisions that you may later regret, but hope that everything turns out well in the end.

At worst, therefore, you are snappy, happy and superficial! You like to think that you are sharp and shrewd, quick to notice changes in your environment, and fast to respond to other people's demeanour. In other words, you can adapt brilliantly to the company you keep; but this can mean that you fail to develop steady inner awareness of your own identity.

Of course you're a natural talker and writer, juggling with ideas, emotions and new projects all the time. Indeed, your brain is always teeming with things to do, but often you carry them out in a careless and inefficient way. You enjoy a 'busy' lifestyle surrounded by stimulating people. Too much peace and quiet gets you down!

In brief, you have the emotional disposition of a spry, cocky city-dweller, living by your wits, eager to learn more and, at times, the life and soul of the party!

Your Folk Memory

You are capable of being highly intuitive, but equally you can be quite deaf to inner promptings. The symbol of Gemini is the Heavenly Twins, representing the spiritual and earthly sides of your nature. You have good access to both twins; but too often the clever, know-all one grabs all the attention, never letting you hear the still, small voice of the spirit within you.

When you can silence your noisy, everyday brain you will find much truth and wisdom. Your intuition will speak to you in signs and symbols: perhaps a geometric shape, a kaleidoscope of colours, a sudden vision resembling a surreal painting. Many Moon-in-Gemini people suffer from insomnia at some stage in their lives; but at other times, your dreams will be sharp, vivid messages from your Unconscious. They will not be obvious, and you must learn to interpret them.

One favourite dream will involve you as the great persuader: a demagogue swaying his audience, perhaps, or a statesman altering the course of history. If you succeed in this task, your Unconscious is basically saying 'Well done!', but if your oratory fails, if the crowd turns against you, there is something wrong with your psyche – something to feel guilty about.

Typical Moon-in-Gemini nightmares involve danger, speed and noises: cars over cliffs, an angry, chanting crowd, and time getting out of sync. But whenever you have an Alice-in-Wonderland dream, vivid with symbols, try on awakening to remember the salient details. There could be a highly significant meaning there.

Links with the Past

Clearly you have spent recent lives learning to adapt to new circumstances. So you have probably lived at times of great change, when old patterns were broken up and new social forces were at work.

There have been many such moments in history: the rise of empires, the breakthrough of new technology, the emigration of people to new countries. There's a special link with the United States, and you could well have been part of the great 19th-century surge westwards. But there have been other periods of ferment in the past few centuries to which you may feel drawn: the Civil War era in England, for instance, or the French Revolution, or the spread of trade in India and the Far East. Trade and education, in particular, are the activities with which you have been associated.

I should think your most recent life on Earth was quite a short while ago. It would be interesting to know whether you died young, no later than your teens, for your Geminian psyche has an air of youthful high spirits which never matured.

Another possibility is that you have just changed – or are about to change – sex. Probably you are coming to the end of a sexual pattern, and will switch over in your next life. This is particularly true if you are male now; by the 21st century you will have incarnated as a girl.

In your present life you are probably mixing with many people whom you have known as acquaintances in earlier lives – people whom you may well have cheated in the past. So it pays to be as generous as possible, giving them the benefit of the doubt if they, in turn, appear to cheat you now.

Links with Sun-Signs

Your Geminian psyche makes you an easy mixer, enjoying the company of a wide variety of other folk. Here's your brief guide to the virtues and faults of your own character, depending on your own Sun-sign. (I've indicated a Moon-in-Gemini celebrity born under each sign.) In the right-hand column you can see how you relate to the various Zodiac people.

Sun-Sign *Your own Character*	*Relating to Others*
Aries Vibrant, egoistic, keen to impress others. You have the gift of oratory, learnt in the past. Example: BETTE DAVIS.	Nice rapport here. You may have known each other in happy circumstances in the past. Always be honest with Aries.
Taurus Nice mixture of charm and stability. Plenty of artistic talent learnt in the past. Have been clever with business. Example: PERRY COMO.	You want to liven up Taurus. Taurus will try to tie you down. Learn practical skills and teach independence and adaptability to Taurus!
Gemini A flowing personality, easy in company. Your big lesson is how to persevere and be reliable. You face a crucial life, deciding your path ahead. Example: DEAN MARTIN.	Instant rapport, but you may tire quickly of each other. Try to work together, sharing enthusiasms. Could have been siblings in previous lives.
Cancer A lively and protective nature, young at heart. Could have an adventurous life, with history repeating itself from a previous life. Example: YUL BRYNNER.	An oddball relationship at times, but positive. You play a child to Cancer's parent. A cosy, perhaps cloying link.
Leo A flashy personality, keen to capture attention. You have to re-learn a lesson you failed in an earlier life. Example: TONY BENNETT.	Excellent mix, as you are both egotists at heart! Could have been sweethearts in a previous incarnation together.

Sun-Sign Your own Character *Relating to Others*

Virgo Nervous, worrying about others, high ideals, a bit of an ascetic. Can recall spiritual wisdom learnt in previous lives. Example: MOTHER TERESA.

A clever combination, so you have probably worked together in the past. Resist the karmic temptation to be critical of each other.

Libra A beauty-loving nature, full of charm and love. A life of continuity – or a deserved rest after lifetimes of problems. Example: BRIGITTE BARDOT.

Real friendship here, though there may not be deep ties. Rather a passive relationship so you must learn strength and courage from each other.

Scorpio Real struggle between spirit and psyche, veering from flip to heavy. Deep search for your inner identity. Example: GOLDIE HAWN.

Can appreciate each other even though you're so different. Almost certainly deep karmic ties between you.

Sagittarius Free-ranging personality, self-reliant and bouncy. Probably a scholar, explorer or gypsy in previous life. Example: KIRK DOUGLAS.

A wonderful friendship is possible here, but lots of arguments. too! Could well have done similar work in different parts of the world in earlier lives together.

Capricorn Bright ideas and hard-headed realism. Could have been architect or engineer in earlier life. Inclined to be too serious in outlook. Example: ROBERT STACK.

Very different in approach to life. You find Capricorn too cautious at times. It's important that you aren't dominated by Capricorn folk.

Sun-Sign   Your own Character   Relating to Others

Aquarius Friendly, open, resourceful: an obvious talent brought through from an earlier life. Good at politics, teaching and sport. Example: JACK NICKLAUS.

Immediate friendship quite possible here, as though you recognize each other from earlier lives together. It is likely that you underwent joint training in the past.

Pisces Sensitive and psychic, easily led. Have been an artist, monk or nun in the past. May be emotionally hurt in this life. Example: dancer ANTOINETTE SIBLEY.

You work with your head, Pisces with the heart. You get angry with their ditheriness. Your aim must be to learn tolerance of each other.

Psyche in Cancer: Moon 90 – 119

Your Emotional Nature

However tough you may be on the surface, with Moon in Cancer you undoubtedly have a soft centre. You are gentle, protective, somewhat shy and cautious, and devoted to your family.

By 'family' I mean anyone with whom you are familiar, anyone whom you want to nurture. This might be people at work, friends and neighbours as well as your actual nearest and dearest. This makes you a cosy, receptive individual – though at worst you can be too clannish, refusing help to people who don't 'belong'.

There's a deeply private side to your nature. You need to withdraw from everyday life – to brood, read, garden or take a long bath! Then you bounce back, full of kindly energy, wanting to involve yourself in other people's doings. This veering to and fro, like the tides, makes you seem a moody person on occasion – indeed, a feminine person, whatever your actual sex may be.

This is the psyche that you have brought from previous lives. It is the clue to your spiritual background – the kind of person you have become in earlier incarnations.

Your Folk Memory
You are much more closely in touch with the psychic world than many people around you. Not only will you have a rich and vivid dream-life; a fair number of your waking hours are spent in day-dreaming, and many of your day-to-day judgments about people are based on inner intuition.

You are particularly sensitive, as I say, to 'family' feelings. Without quite realizing it, you are able to discern those you have known in previous lives – and those that are strangers. At first meeting, you'll know whether a person 'belongs' or not. In this respect, you're a guardian of tribal consciousness. You are the watchman at the door, glad to be hospitable but still wary of any thing – or person – out of the ordinary.

Many of your dreams will revolve around this concept of homeliness. It's important for you to have favourite imaginary places where you feel peaceful; and in some dreams you may go back to real places that you have known in the past.

Nightmares challenge your sense of security. They could involve the fear of losing a loved one. You are a deeply possessive person. If, in your dreams, you cling too passionately to things you love, your Unconsciousness is telling you that, like a good mother, you must allow those in your care to grow up and move away.

You, more than most, have access to the creative power of the imagination. By constantly forming an ideal image in your mind's eye, you are in effect making it easier for that image to become real in everyday life.

Links with the Past
You are likely to have incarnated with the same group of

friends – oh yes, and enemies! – that you have known in previous lives. With your family in particular you are likely to have strong ties – for better or worse! Your mother, most of all, will have had an indelible impression on the formation of your psyche. (This applies even if you don't like her, or if she disappeared when you were young. Her very absence will have shaped your inner nature in an inimitable way.)

You've been developing along a homely, close-focused line of development in the recent past. You have been learning how to be kind, caring for others, responsive to the needs of the young, the weak and the poor. You may still be fighting this trend, trying to be more independent, but undoubtedly some of the Cancerian virtues will have been incorporated.

It's quite likely that your Key Life, the one most relevant to your current existence, took place a long time ago – perhaps back in the Middle Ages, ancient Egypt or early China. Very probably you have spent time in India, also in a humble capacity in Catholic Europe. In this present life you are being given the opportunity to rediscover the simple truths of warm togetherness that you absorbed many centuries ago.

Countries that are specially linked with Cancer are Scotland, the Indian sub-continent and many parts of Africa.

As you meditate on your previous lives, you may well get a flash of homesteads, plain rural life, and, above all, an aura of family love. You have been a settler in the past. Your task now, as then, is to make people, plants and animals at home in your presence. It is very likely that if you're an animal lover, the same spirit will keep reincarnating, in one pet animal after another, in the course of your lifetime.

Links with Spirit

I've tried to portray you as a soft-centred individual, wanting to be friends but inevitably a bit cautious at first. In this section you can see a glimpse of your rounded character – Spirit and Psyche combined – depending on your Sun-sign. I

mention a celebrity for each combination, to give an idea how
the two sides of nature work together. Also included is a note
about how you, as a Moon-in-Cancer type, relate to people
born under different Zodiac signs.

Sun-Sign	*Your own Character*	*Relating to Others*
Aries	At best a fine balance between action and sympathy, at worst a stormy petrel. A person of power and responsibility in earlier Key Life. Example: SPENCER TRACY.	Different attitudes to life but you can still appreciate each other. Aries may have hurt you in the past, but don't try to get even now.
Taurus	A wonderfully reassuring nature, with deep instinctual sympathy. May be embedded in the past too much. An old-fashioned realist. Example: DR BENJAMIN SPOCK.	Ideal combination for family partners. Lots of deep understanding. Could well have grown together through many lives in the past.
Gemini	Interesting mixture of ancient and modern! An old heart with a young-in-mind outlook on life. This life may be a 'second-chance' one to correct earlier faults. Example: ENOCH POWELL.	Gemini is too busy and lively for the likes of you! Try to reach a happy compromise but don't be surprised if Gemini tries to cheat you!
Cancer	Spirit and psyche combined in one	Clearly a fine match. The trouble is that you could be

Sun-Sign Your own Character Relating to Others

powerful aura. A busy and over-possessive person at times. Probably been a woman for many lives. Example: OLIVIA DE HAVILLAND.

too moody towards each other. May well have been women friends for many lives.

Leo Highly imaginative type who likes to show off! Very powerful impact, due to wide experience in past lives. Example: ROMAN POLANSKI.

Enjoyable mix, though you tend to pour cold water on Leo's bright ideas! Good for raising a family.

Virgo Shrewd, caring, keen to explore the past. Have been good at management, accounts etc in the past. Example: ANTONIA FRASER.

Workaday understanding of each other. Easily could have had the same religious training in the Middle Ages.

Libra Charming, sunny disposition, born to communicate happiness. Has learnt the hard way how to be fair and merciful. Example: JULIE ANDREWS.

Attractive couple that can spend many happy years together. Libra helps calm you down. Good for artistic partnerships (which you may have had in past lives).

Scorpio Very emotional creature, with many gifts and hang-ups from previous lives. Apt to get lost in a jungle of emotions. Example: singer AYSHEA BROUGH.

Liable to have powerful ties but too sensitive for comfort. Love can switch to hate at a moment's notice.

Sun-Sign   Your own Character   Relating to Others

Sagittarius Can draw on the past to give inspiration to new projects. Interesting blend of tradition and modernity. Example: Indian boy-wonder mystic JI MAHARAJ.

Your task is to provide an emotional base where Sagittarius can feel at home. Can be a fruitful combination.

Capricorn Deeply conservative nature, with spirit and psyche flowing in a mature and balanced way. Indicates a rounded soul who can handle responsibility. Example: actor JOHN THAW.

One of the best possible Zodiac combinations. Can indicate soul-mates, people who have spent many lifetimes together in the past.

Aquarius Contradictory impulses. The adventurer who needs a nest, the freedom-lover who wants to belong. You could be breaking free after many lifetimes bound to a particular dogma. Example: TELLY SAVALAS.

Intriguing mixture of moodiness and cool reason. Bound to be disputes. Your task is to provide love without possessiveness! A hard lesson!

Pisces Intensely free-floating and escapist, controlled by the emotions. Very powerful feelings, probably developed in very sensual former lives. Need to find peace of mind. Example: LIZA MINNELLI.

Lots of empathy, not much commonsense. Your lives are full of unfinished emotional business. You must learn to gain control over yourself before the relationship can truly flourish.

Psyche in Leo: Moon 120 – 149

Your Emotional Nature

Inside you there's a warm, glowing need to be loved. In order to thrive, you need to live in a constant aura of affection. Denied this, you soon become bitter and tetchy.

So your response to life is large, sunny and wholesome. You have a childlike capacity to be pleased with simple delights. Your heart goes out to anything that is charming or sweet – but like the sun itself, your mood soon droops if a single dark cloud appears.

You can see that a Leo psyche is born innocent rather than worldly-wise; but of course it must learn to become mature and balanced. The undeveloped Moon-in-Leo person is like a spoilt child, full of tantrums when things go wrong. You must develop the patience to put up with second-best, to be alone if need be, and, most difficult of all, to accept that some people may never like you!

You love the fine things of life: luxuries, holidays of all kinds, flirtations and gifts and happy laughter. At your best, you can project all these lovable qualities into the lives of others; at worst, you want to keep them all to yourself.

Your Folk Memory

This liking for wealth, coupled with your own personal pride, can prevent you from leading a true life of the spirit. If you are obsessed with your immediate needs, you leave no time for the deeper, subtler side of your nature.

But most Leo psyches, especially when happy, have a remarkably truthful insight. They *know*, as soon as they meet someone, whether goodness shines out. And their dreams have a bonny optimism, at times, that comes straight from heaven.

For the part of our Folk Memory that attracts you most strongly is the time when mankind is at ease. Favourite dreams will centre on midsummer sport, dalliance, fun and games. You will enjoy being the champion athlete, Cinderella at the ball, the musical star in the spotlight, the body beautiful on the beach. When you can dream happily of sunshine holidays and admiring glances, then all's well with your psyche. But when things go wrong – when someone kicks sand in your face, so to speak – your Unconscious is telling you that you are not being true to your Leo psyche.

Every so often you'll have glimpses of past lives, but beware of deceiving yourself. More than most people, can you be swayed by flattery and snob appeal; and it's tempting for you to believe that your dream about Versailles or Cleopatra must have been a personal memory, surely.

Typical Moon-in-Leo nightmares could involve loneliness and panic: the fear of getting lost in dark corridors, of never finding the bright lights again. There could also be a recurrent bad dream about a rival – someone who unfairly takes your place. It could be the fear of someone stealing your loved one – or, more deeply, the dread that the kindly God who rules your inner universe will turn out the light and disappear.

Links with the Past

Anyone with a Leo psyche has enjoyed some measure of good luck, affection and happiness in the past. You will have basked in someone's love, or shared someone's glory, or been given a holiday from the serious business of spiritual evolution.

Indeed, your present life could be along similar lines. You are particularly likely to meet sex partners in this life who have set you alight in previous incarnations. Sexual love resembles a bright flame, glamorous but full of danger, too. Leo psyches are specially prone to sexual karma: being spurned by someone whom you rejected earlier, being attracted to someone whom you know you must not touch.

Leo is specially linked with France and Italy and the Latin peoples generally. It has obvious links, too, with Central America and possibly ancient Persia. These are countries where you could have developed your Leo qualities. If you have unique feelings of love for the Mediterranean shores, then you are almost certainly being drawn back to places where you have passed happy times, long ago. Certain areas of Greece, too, come under the spell of Leo (otherwise known as Apollo).

Special gifts which may have been developed in the past are linked with entertainment, singing and dancing, and, more broadly, with personal command: the ability to get eyes to turn in your direction. You are probably still learning karmic lessons here, mainly about the wise use of this inner magnetism.

Links with Spirit

With your Moon-in-Leo nature you have a lovely sunny disposition, a golden framework for the rest of your soul's attributes. Here's a brief guide to psyche and spirit combined, showing how your Leo qualities vary according to your Zodiac Sun-sign. (I include 12 celebrities, one for each Sun-sign, to show how the influences work.) Also given are the ways you relate to people born under the various signs.

Sun-Sign Your own Character	Relating to Others
Aries Enterprising character, able to command an audience. Bound to have been a leader in earlier times. Can be too proud. Example: PETER USTINOV.	Friendly but competitive. Blazing rows soon forgotten. Could have been male rivals in previous period.
Taurus Determined type, pleased with oneself but practical too. Must learn to relax. Will have held strong views in previous	Two strong characters who can be stubborn towards each other. Have met in this life to resolve old differences. Compromise needed!

Sun-Sign   Your own Character   Relating to Others

life. Example: JOHNNY
MILLER.

Gemini Warm-hearted
extrovert with charm and
an inquisitive nature. A
Peter Pan type facing
problems evaded in the
past. Example: JACQUES
COUSTEAU.

Lovely flow of appreciation
between you. A partnershp
that never wants to grow
old. Could well have been
soul-mates over many lives.

Cancer All-round family
type, more private than
you seem. Excellently
poised to make a valuable
contribution in this life,
thanks to training in the
past. Example: RINGO
STARR.

Excellent mix for husband
and wife. Have probably
been in the same 'family' for
many incarnations. In this
life you must wake up
Cancer.

Leo An overpowering
presence at times – in
business and personal
relations. You must resist
the temptation to think
you're God Almighty!
Example: LUCILLE BALL.

Obviously you can give
much happiness to each
other. Beware of burning
each other up through too
much passion.

Virgo Apparently a show-
off, but a puritan at
heart! Have developed a
warm heart in recent lives
– now you must learn
discrimination. Example:
TWIGGY.

Can be many irritations
beneath the surface. Virgo
wants to act as your
conscience, and could have
been a pain in the neck in
the past.

Libra Someone who thrives

You have every reason to

Sun-Sign Your own Character Relating to Others

on charm and affection. Your greatest gift is the ability to make others happy. Probably had job as judge, master of ceremonies or painter in the past. Example: PIERRE TRUDEAU.

enjoy each other's company. Through efforts in the past you should have a pleasant life together now.

Scorpio Complex personality, very proud, with a chip on your shoulder. A soldier, harsh parent or scientist in the past. Biggest problem: self-pity. Example: VERONICA LAKE.

There could be a battle royal between you. Try to forgive and forget. A life when old karma could be made worse, not better.

Sagittarius Often spells success in life. It's as though you've been released from a burden and can be free again. Example: EMERSON FITTIPALDI.

A marvellously creative partnership, very show-bizzy and extrovert. It may be that you are old pals who meet every so often.

Capricorn A character on a power-kick! You could make a wonderful managing director – or gangster! Biggest task is being fair to everyone. Example: DAVID BOWIE.

Not bad for business, but a tricky combination in love. Your job is to give warmth to stuffy old Capricorn.

Aquarius One of the noblest mixtures in the

This can work surprisingly well! It's a relationship of

Sun-Sign   Your own Character   Relating to Others

Zodiac: gifts of art and science, warmth and humaneness. Essential to use these gifts for a serious, altruistic way. Example: JACK LEMMON.

great hope and affection and mutual respect. Could have been courtiers in previous life.

Pisces A lovely, in-built gaiety but also a childlike determination not to grow up! You can fool yourself, and be fooled by others. Example: LEE MARVIN.

Good combination, so long as you're kind to each other. Otherwise Pisces will deceive you, and you'll try to rule the roost.

Psyche in Virgo: Moon 150 – 179

Your Emotional Nature

Yours is a small-scale response to life. Whatever your outer qualities may be, inwardly you have a neat, crisp demeanour – at best, the heart of an angel, at worst, the soul of a filing clerk!

Let me explain. It's natural for your psyche to look for the best in everything, but in doing so you use such a sharp, critical intelligence that you resemble a librarian at times, slotting everyone into their right classification. It's a self-aware nature, conscious of your own reactions to life, a bit shy where other people are concerned and apt to feel guilty about things that aren't your fault. But you're a great self-improver, wanting to aim high, wanting to do better next time.

Emotionally, you keep thinking you're a failure, although actually you may be a winner every time.

This constant inner examining can lead to fussiness at times. You may be fussy about the food you eat, the company you keep and even the ideas that you allow into your brain. You're a worrier, too. You worry about your health, your wealth and what the neighbours might think. As you well know, these are admirable virtues so long as they don't become obsessions; but the trouble with the Virgoan psyche is that it tends to be wrapped up a little too obsessively with its own concerns.

Well, that's not quite true. You are certainly a self-contained individual, with a kind of glass bubble around your heart to keep strangers at bay; but this doesn't stop you from caring desperately about other people, their welfare, and what you can do to help.

In short, you're a private person in a public world.

Your Folk Memory

There are two archetypes close to the Virgoan soul: the craftsman and the monk. One represents your attention to detail (so that you can't see the wood for the trees); and the other, contrariwise, your ability to serve God and Man, to marry idealism with practicality.

So there are two kinds of Moon-in-Virgo people: those with closed, workaday minds and the rest of you, who, at times at least, possess an extraordinarily clear vision side by side with your usual earthly worries.

Your dream-life is likely to be a fascinating jumble of itsy-bitsy panic and true insight! Many of your dreams will revolve around the concept of purity: getting things right, perfecting a skill, ensuring cleanliness and good order and always defending, if need be, your integrity. For the part of our Folk Memory that attracts you is the need for discrimination. This can take several typical forms. There is the savant, the one who knows the difference between wise and foolish knowledge. There is the adept, the one who has learnt through experience the right way to do anything – run a business, farm the countryside, deal with problems of all kinds. And there's the disciple, the one who is learning through personal endeavour how to discriminate between good and evil.

Your dream-life hero will be one of these, suitably disguised. This could be the good neighbour, the hospital nurse, the laboratory scientist. If such a hero creates smiling gratitude, then your psyche is at peace with itself. If, on the other hand, your hero is self-important, hectoring others to do better, your psyche is uneasy and worried. It is telling you to change yourself for the better: in particular, to be more humble in your attitudes to others.

Links with the Past

Of all the signs, Virgo and Pisces are most associated with Christianity; and of all the characters in the gospel story, none is more typically Virgoan than Martha, the sister who slaved away while her pretty Piscean sister Mary sat still, adoring Jesus.

Your Virgoan psyche is bound to have been honed and polished through a good few Christian incarnations in the past 2000 years. Almost certainly you'll have been a monk or nun or friar or priest several times over, absorbing into your soul the unique combination of poverty, chastity and the greater glory of God.

These virtues are not exclusively Christian, of course. You will also have spent some time as a Buddhist or possibly, though less probably, as a Muslim. Nor are they exclusively religious. The quiet and homely Virgoan approach to life can be happily developed in domestic surroundings, welfare work or peasant husbandry. Any vivid glimpses you receive of life as a servant or labourer in the old days could well have a ring of truth.

Virgoan countries are Switzerland, Denmark and Holland and indeed, in this connection, all of Protestant Northern Europe. The Bible Belt in America, too, has been a training ground for many a Virgoan psyche.

Training, discipline and renunciation are wholesome but not happy virtues. Many people with Virgo strong in their souls will have undergone sadness and deprivation in the past, so that today, as a karmic legacy, they may be inhibited in certain ways: sexually, perhaps, but also in general emotional development. So you may well encounter people who have cramped you in earlier lives – or whom you, in turn, have thwarted. You are probably still working out the final balance sheet of Puritanism, and people who seem to flaunt strong feelings before you are unconsciously getting their own back for the rigorous discipline you imposed on them, centuries ago.

Links with Spirit

Your Moon-in-Virgo psyche is like glass: apparently not there until people knock into it! It allows other parts of your nature, especially spirit, to shine through, while it stays privately in the background, known only to yourself and close friends. Here's your guide to the virtues and faults of your whole character, depending on your own Sun-sign, with a Moon-in-Virgo celebrity as an example. In the right-hand column you can see how you relate to various Zodiac people.

Sun-Sign Your own Character *Relating to Others*

Aries A shrewd loudmouth, blowing hot but thinking coldly. You could have been an engineer, soldier or administrator who was denied the opportunity to command. Example: NIKITA KHRUSHCHEV.

Not an easy match. You come from different ends of the psychological spectrum, and have plenty to learn from each other.

Taurus A patient, conscientious type, applying wise lessons learnt in the past. A

Nice combination. You will work well together. There may be too much one-track thinking, and not enough

Sun-Sign   Your own Character   Relating to Others

tendency to get stuck in a   experimentation.
rut. Example: QUEEN
JULIANA OF THE
NETHERLANDS.

Gemini An inventive mind,   A nervy, clever relationship.
tending to be resourceful   Not a lot of warmth or
rather than intuitive.   sympathy, but a respect for
Almost certainly a   each other. Good for
teacher, salesman or   learning skills from each
negotiator in past lives.   other in this life.
Example: HENRY
KISSINGER.

Cancer Good mixture of   A pleasant and homely
intelligence and   mixture, who may well have
sympathy. Almost   been quiet friends for a long
certainly a dominant   time. A comfy link.
woman in recent key life.
Example: GINA
LOLLOBRIGIDA.

Leo A talented individual   Not an easy friendship to
keen to display your   sustain. Be careful not to
skills. Warm in public,   hold Leo back too much.
self-critical in private.   Could have been master and
Now's the life to enjoy   servant in previous life.
yourself. Example: opera
singer JANET BAKER.

Virgo Highly self-contained   Obviously you can have a
person able to concentrate   quietly happy relationship.
hard. Not an easy person   Gentle growth of the spirit
to know. Almost certainly   is clearly possible here.
a figure of authority in
the Church at some time.

Sun-Sign   Your own Character   Relating to Others
   Example: SEAN
CONNERY.

Libra Cool sweetness, delicate judgment. Could have trained in the Law – or been chastened by punishment in a recent life. Example: DEBORAH KERR.

Good links here, because you do not seek to dominate each other. Probably have co-operated well in recent incarnations – in China?

Scorpio Cool but terribly determined, possibly gripped still by passions from the past. You can be too harsh in your judgments of others. Example: KATHARINE HEPBURN.

Beware of being bullied by Scorpio. Almost certainly there has been trouble in the past. Now's the time to be honest with yourselves.

Sagittarius Curious mixture of liveliness and acerbity, as you can be bold and shy at same time! Could have been doctor, scientist, preacher. Example: SAMMY DAVIS JNR.

Could have been friends a long time ago, then gone your separate ways. Now's the time to compare notes again!

Capricorn Ultra-practical, dry-as-dust, kindly but dogmatic. The born headmaster, statesman, corporation executive, then as now. Example: HELMUT SCHMIDT.

Good business links, but together you lack warmth. This could be the end of the road for a while. You need to journey in new directions.

Sun-Sign   Your own Character   Relating to Others

Aquarius The nearest the
Zodiac can get to Mr
Brains! You have moved
fast along a path of
mental development.
Now you must branch
into fresh pastures.
Example: GEORGES
SIMENON.

Respectful and fond, but no
great passion here. But you
can share great ideals – and
enjoy putting the world to
rights!

Pisces Dreamer and critic
combined! Your head
says one thing, your heart
another. Liable to deceive
yourself – the result of
fooling others in the past.
Example: EDWARD
KENNEDY.

Although very different
creatures, you can still live
happily together. You could
have had an Abelard-and-
Heloise love affair in the
Middle Ages.

Psyche in Libra: Moon 180 – 209

Your Emotional Nature

Within your breast there's a sweet and agreeable nature that
longs to find harmony around you. Whereas your opposite
number, the Arean psyche, has an aggressive response to life,
yours is peaceful and full of tenderness.

Instead of being egotistical you much prefer to identify with
a group. This may be the family, your circle of friends, the
nation at large – whichever it is, you are more interested in 'us'
than 'me'. This applies particularly to personal relationships
such as love affairs or marriage. What your partner thinks of
you, for better or worse, is more important than what you
think of yourself.

Obviously you can be too passive at times, agreeing with
others when you should be much more determined and selfish.

And you can be so dithery in your reactions that you never make up your mind. At worst, you are always responding to the latest developments instead of taking the broad view of events.

You have good taste. You know what suits you, and you are interested in the arts, fashion, decor, literature and the theatre. This is a predominantly feminine kind of psyche, wanting to evade problems and harsh conditions and seek always the pleasant, easy and harmonious side of life.

Your Folk Memory

With your delicacy of outlook and subtlety of inner response, you have good rapport with the psychic side of life. You can perceive the real meaning behind people's actions, and you are particularly good at reading the public mood, sensing the next shift in opinion or fashion.

The part of our Folk Memory that attracts you is the urge towards togetherness. Man is a gregarious creature, needing to share his emotions with others. And in your dreams and meditations you are likely to tap this age-old desire to gather in friendship, exchange views and ideas, and, above all, form one-to-one partnerships.

At a simple level, favourite dreams will be romances where boy meets girl and together they live happily ever after. More complexly, your dreams could involve yearning for complete-ness: two different people or lifestyles which really ought to be joined together. The happy-ever-after version indicates that your psyche is satisfied with life; but if the other kind of dream predominates, your psyche is crying out for more peace and affection in daily life.

Typical nightmares revolve around loneliness, the fear of being cut adrift or excluded from social gatherings, and the pain of making the wrong choice – and being unable to change your mind! A cheerful company of friends, at ease among themselves, is your idea of heaven – and when you experience this kind of dream, you are deeply in touch with the wellsprings of community life.

Links with the Past
Clearly you have not been a loner in past lives. Instead you have been learning how to mix amicably with others. You may have been put into a weak position out of karma, so that you can appreciate what it's like to be bullied. You may have been made dithery, so you can appreciate the terrible consequences of being too hasty in your judgments.

Where could all this have happened? Obviously anywhere, but the countries most associated with the Libran psyche are Japan and China. Both Buddhism and Taoism are highly Libran religions, concentrating as they do on good social behaviour, reverence for all life, and – in Buddhism especially – the sacrifice of personal ambition to attain *nirvana*.

I should think you have spent a good many lives in the Far East, perhaps quite recently but, since Asian lifestyles have remained the same for several thousand years, possibly a long time ago.

Your Key Life was certainly spent among close friends. Possibly you managed to turn enemies into friends, or found how to live happily among strangers. All these skills in handling humans, slowly learnt in the past, are now innate gifts of your psyche.

Other times and places where you could have incarnated are 18th-century Europe (especially France and the Austro-Hungarian Empire), the Indian Raj, Regency England and Sweden at any time.

Links with Spirit
You're capable of being the best mixer in the Zodiac, if you give your psyche half a chance. But this depends partly on what kind of spirit you've got. Here's your sign-by-sign guide to the way your Libran psyche combines with your Zodiac

Sun-sign, with a celebrity given as an example in each case. On the right-hand side, you can see how you get on with other Sun-sign people.

Sun-Sign Your own character	*Relating to Others*
Aries Charming in yourself, but a firebrand in your career. Tend to blow hot and cold. Still to learn the lesson of emotional peace. Example: CHARLES CHAPLIN.	A real Tarzan-and-Jane relationship. Could well have been husband and wife in past lives. Make sure that you learn to reach a compromise.
Taurus A marvellously relaxing figure, sweet in company and still capably down-to-earth. Were a successful businessman and lover in past life. Example: HENRY FONDA.	Good links, because you both respond to the planet of love Venus. Could have been artists together in the past.
Gemini Sweet and gentle, finds it very hard to be fully adult! Probably female in recent lives. May use trick emotions to win hearts and minds. Example: TONY CURTIS.	Excellent links, among the best in the Zodiac. Almost certainly friends for a long time – but you may put too much trust in little Gemini!
Cancer Sensitive, deeply concerned with feelings of love and togetherness. Rather moody yourself, but talented in the arts. Example: INGMAR BERGMAN.	Just the right amount of emotional tension. Probably have been in the same family in the past.

Sun-Sign   Your own Character   Relating to Others

Leo Charming, pleased with yourself, wanting to win affection but inclined to be too proud. Could have been a dramatic actress. Example: FIDEL CASTRO.

Every chance of success, for you have easy access to each other's hearts. Surely have been lovers in the past.

Virgo Amiable but undramatic combination. You are in a standing-still sort of life, biding your time, acting a middle-man to others around you. Example: FRED McMURRAY.

Friendly without being wild about each other. You're good companions, and are slowly building up links.

Libra Powerful Libran, able to put your artistic and personal skills to practical use. Partnership is the crucial aspect of life, and you're in search of your soul-mate in this life. Example: NANA MOUSKOURI.

Obviously happy links, as you're a popular couple among friends. One of you is following in the footsteps of the other.

Scorpio An amiable nature, much tougher than you seem. A balanced character, perhaps a lawyer in the past. Example: ALISTAIR COOKE.

Danger that you'll be dominated by Scorpio. It's your job to see that Scorpio does not go to silly extremes.

Sagittarius Taste allied to

A splendid mix, for

Sun-Sign Your own Character	*Relating to Others*
adventure. An intriguing character, very talented and communicative. Usually an extrovert person with many gifts from an earlier life. Example: WALT DISNEY.	Sagittarius brings out your cheerfulness. Good for making a fresh start after karmic debts have been repaid.
Capricorn Gentle but determined, with a history of politics and administration behind you. If you are weak, you may be the slow coach who gets there in the end. Example: ANWAR SADAT.	Large difference in temperament. You can teach Capricorn to mix mercy with justice – maybe a reverse from previous lives.
Aquarius Charm allied to intelligence. Definitely a life of continuity, building on success in the past. Example: VALERY GISCARD D'ESTAING.	A lively couple full of ideas. Sociable, plenty of taste. You have ironed out most of the difficulties between you.
Pisces Highly sensitive and imaginative, with direct access to the unconciousness. At worst a ditherer – at best, an artist going straight to the heart. Example: RUDOLPH NUREYEV.	You are sensitive in separate ways. You'll find Pisces too moody at times while Pisces finds you too trivial. So you still have plenty to learn.

Psyche in Scorpio: Moon 210 – 239

Your Emotional Nature
Scorpio is a complex, many-layered Zodiac sign, and so your

response to life is equally enigmatic. Whatever your outward manner may be, inwardly you can be fierce, devoted, moody, self-critical and sarcastic – all at the same time!

You can be a most secretive creature, as far as your personal feelings are concerned. You don't wear your heart on your sleeve, but enjoy knowing secrets about others. Sometimes you can keep the truth from yourself, so you suddenly wake up to find that you have changed your mind overnight.

Emotionally you are possessive to the point of jealousy. Once you commit your heart, you put all your determination into that relationship. But, as I say, secretly you may build up resentment, dislike and even revenge to the point that, overnight, your feelings are never the same again.

Your response to life is rarely trivial. In your heart of hearts, your instinct is to take life seriously, to deepen the current of emotion rather than make it more shallow. In your habits of thought and feeling, you are a strong-minded, rather obsessive person tending to go to extremes rather than take the middle path.

Your Folk Memory

People with Moon-in-Scorpio have the knack of treating subtle inner intuition as ordinary commonsense. You are far more deeply in touch with your Unconscious than you realize.

Because of this, you are likely to have much richer dreams than many other people. In your dream-life you may well perceive the occasional echo of a past life, and also be closely in touch with the Collective Unconscious shared by all of us.

The part of our Folk Memory that most appeals to you is the crisis: the life-or-death moment when a supreme effort is demanded. Your heroes are likely to be doctors, sea-captains, pilots, adventurers – anyone who must take a calculated risk in order to escape from disaster. Possibly you will see yourself in a former incarnation involved in a struggle for survival, or you may relive the myths of Wagner, Tolkien and the Brothers

Grimm. Your nightmares could be cruel and sadistic, for within your psyche there is a knot of emotion that can manifest one moment as inspiration and the next as blind rage.

Some people's psyches are mild and everyday. Yours, on the other hand, is a powerful instrument for change. It is constantly urging you, through guilt and self-criticism, to do better, turn over a new leaf or turn your back on the past. Rarely will you have peaceful dreams, for your psyche is permanently trying to make you take the next fateful step in your journey of spiritual evolution.

Links with the Past

You'll gather that the Scorpio psyche brings a greater load of responsibility from the past than any other Zodiac sign. Of course, it's perfectly possible for you to have a happy life – but not a meaningless one. You have too many obligations for that.

Your last lives would have been strenuous and effortful, during which a great deal of old karma will have been reaped and new karma sown. The people whom you meet in this life are almost certainly old friends and enemies you have met many times before. And because the Scorpio psyche is bound up with large masses of unresolved emotion, you will almost certainly be drawn back to places where this emotion built up in the past: a house where a tense relationship developed, a town where you spent a dramatic lifetime, even a country where you had crucial dealings, long ago.

Countries linked with Scorpio are the Arabic lands of the Middle East, Norway, possibly Morocco and Bavaria. Cities said to be governed by this Zodiac sign are Liverpool, New Orleans, Washington DC and Newcastle.

More broadly, the Islamic religion is highly Scorpionic, so you could well have been a Muslim in the past. Other appropriate cultures would be the Counter-Reformation in Europe, the Aztecs in Central America and Jewish life almost anywhere in the last 2000 years.

In personal terms, you spent your Key Life developing your courage, staying power and emotional loyalty. There could well have been a kind of Armageddon in your heart between good and evil. People will have put fierce pressures on you, and in this life you are tempted to reply again to these pressures – out of gratitude to good people, out of revenge to others.

Links with Spirit

You know well that you're a bit of a loner at times, mixing with caution and, once you've found a new friend, testing this friendship to see whether it's worthwhile. Here's your guide to the virtues and faults of your total character, depending on your own Sun-sign, with a Moon-in-Scorpio celebrity as an example. In the right-hand column you can see how you relate to people born under various signs.

Sun-Sign Your own Character	Relating to Others
Aries Apparently an extrovert but an introvert underneath. Person of power who is trying to release yourself from the shackles of the past. Example: DAVID FROST.	Battle of willpower in this relationship. Your task is to control the excesses of Aries, but Aries is trying to open you up! Quite a battle!
Taurus Very solid, dependable type who has been trained in a particular discipline (military or religious) in the past. Must now learn how to adapt without letting go. Example: film-maker FRED ZINNEMAN.	Great love-hate relationship. You keep your feet on the ground, while Scorpio is full of ideals. Can be a very fertile connection, helping the world move ahead.

| *Sun-Sign Your own Character* | *Relating to Others* |

Gemini Complete contradiction between inner and outer self. Obviously you are trying to reconcile two distinct paths travelled at different times in the past. Example: JOHN WAYNE.

Each admires and despises the other! Like Cain and Abel – and you could well have been brothers in previous lives.

Cancer Highly emotional combination, and powerful links with previous lives. Strong emphasis on medicine, healing and motherhood as talents learnt in the past. Example: JONATHAN MILLER.

Fierce, loyal, make-or-break relationship. There could be passions aroused that will take many lives to live down.

Leo Difficult temperament to handle, as you want adoration but don't always give much in return. You are learning the lesson of the wise use of love. Example: LIONEL BART.

Attracted to each other, but with an undercurrent of animosity. You hate the Leo propensity to flirt. Perhaps you like each other too much – so cool it!

Virgo Shy but stubborn, with high ideals. Certainly a religious or political background. You are learning a special skill in this life, not easily

The union works well if the other person is prepared to be meek! You are only happy if you aim high together, leading lives of service.

Sun-Sign   Your own Character   Relating to Others

shared with others.
Example: JEAN-LOUIS
BARRAULT.

Libra Apparently easy-
going, but tough inside.
Could have been a
samurai, diplomat,
propagandist or spy.
Example: GEORGE RAFT.

Highly disparate characters
with much to learn from
each other. Libra will leave
unless you are kind.

Scorpio You're certain that
you have a great destiny
to fulfil – and so you have.
This is a make-or-break
life when you strive to your
utmost. Example:
HOWARD BAKER.

Excellent links, but you can
still clash dangerously unless
you are prepared to forgive
and forget.

Sagittarius A person of
intense enthusiasms,
remarkable stamina.
You can put hard work in
the past to good account
now. Example: DOUGLAS
FAIRBANKS JNR.

A fascinating relationship if
it ever gets off the ground!
You're inclined to hold
Sagittarius back.

Capricorn Perhaps the
toughest combination in
the Zodiac. Clearly a leader
in the past. You'd like to
be leader, but circum-
stances may be against you.
Example: ETHEL MERMAN.

Very businesslike link! At
best, an honourable and
loving union now – but at
worst, you deserve each
other, getting back now
what you gave last time!

| *Sun-Sign* | *Your own Character* | *Relating to Others* |

Aquarius A revolutionary still bound by your past. Inquisitive, proud, arrogant at times. You want to unearth secrets you had to keep hidden in a previous life. Example: HELEN GURLEY BROWN.

You feel life, Aquarius theorizes about it. You will find the Aquarian cool too cold for comfort.

Pisces Artistic, psychic, either a saint or an escapist. Very drawn to the sea, music, religion. Probably a monk or nun in past lives. Example: GEORGE HARRISON.

It works best if you give Pisces freedom instead of insecurity. Try to forgive each other's moods.

Psyche in Sagittarius: Moon 240 – 269

Your Emotional Nature

Of all the psyches in the Zodiac, yours is the most robust and extrovert. However you may appear on the outside, inwardly you have a warm, zestful heart that is capable of bringing any party to life.

This air of bonhomie stems straight from your Moon-in-Sagittarius psyche. Your natural response to life is friendly, inquisitive and yet clearly independent. Although you like most people, and are curious about them, you are not a possessive person yourself, nor, by the same token, do you want to be possessed by them. You treasure your freedom above anything.

People find you an approachable type, easy to chat to. You, in your turn, have little snobbery, as you enjoy mixing with a wide variety of individuals. If anything, you're attracted to people who come from a different background or country than your own; and as far as your own travel is concerned, you long to fly to the furthest horizons.

It's a restless psyche, constantly on the move, needing new enthusiasms to keep it awake. You can be a bit fickle in your moods, abruptly dropping plans for no good reason. And you can also be quite argumentative, tossing outrageous remarks into company just for the fun of it.

Your Folk Memory
If one thinks of intuition as sharp, piercing insights, then you are not a notably intuitive person. But you possess another kind of vision: the ability to see the wide panorama, the view from the top of the mountain.

Your psyche, above all others, can make connections. You can see what several apparently separate ideas have, in fact, in common; and you are good at discerning the rise and fall of themes through history. As a result, you are not psychic like a clairvoyant; but you can be as wise as the wizard Merlin.

The part of our Folk Memory that you will tap in dreams and meditations refers to our ancestral migrations: the surge of people and ideas across the continents. The caravan on the move, the trade ships sailing away, the rise of a new prophet from afar – these are the *déjà vu* images that will flood your consciousness at times. Your hero will be the traveller, the man who brings the glad news, the individualist who follows his own morality rather than that of the crowd. Sometimes, when you identify happily with this archetype, your psyche is clearly happy, too; but at other times, when your hero feels trapped or lacking in confidence, your psyche is expressing its own frustration with your dull and inadequate day-to-day life.

Your nightmares could involve claustrophobia, imprisonment or injustice. To be denied air, sunlight and the freedom to make your own friends is to threaten the vitality of your Sagittarian psyche.

Links with the Past

Clearly you've spent a good many lifetimes learning how to be self-reliant in body and mind. This will have meant experiences as an outcast, a traveller, and also as a thinker developing his own ideas.

Your psyche has learnt how to manage without a cosy family, a secure city-wall or a dogma handed down by the priests on high. Sometimes this will have been painful, sometimes exhilarating, but by now the lessons will have been incorporated – partly, at least – into your soul.

Throughout history there have been many chances to develop your Sagittarian psyche. You could have been a cowboy, sailor, merchant or gypsy; member of a theatrical troupe or diplomatic mission; an émigré, deserter or orphan; or, at an intellectual level, an early scientist or alchemist. Any lifestyle that developed your taste for travel and speculation would have been appropriate.

These lives could have been spent anywhere, for the whole point of the Sagittarian psyche is its internationalism. You could have been – long ago, no doubt – a bushman, Aborigine or nomad tribesman. More recently, you could have roamed Europe or Asia in search of enlightenment. But the continent most linked with Sagittarius is North America, and I'm sure that in the past few centuries you'll have been part of the great trek west.

During these explorations you may have picked up some difficult karma. You may have been irresponsible, leaving people whom you should have protected, running away from enterprises that could have been nurtured. But on the whole your Sagittarian psyche represents a break from the past. You have the chance to make a fresh start; and in doing so, to help others towards a new vision.

Links with Spirit

Your Moon-in-Sagittarius psyche is the friendliest in the Zodiac; and being adaptable it can fit in with most other personalities. Here's your guide to the virtues and faults of your whole character, depending on your own Sun-sign, with a Moon-in-Sagittarius celebrity as an example. In the right-hand column you can see how you relate to various Zodiac people.

Sun-Signs Your own Character	*Relating to Others*
Aries Direct, experimental, very enthusiastic. Could have been a sportsman, traveller, trader in the past – or itinerant preacher. Example: KINGSLEY AMIS.	Both of you relish freedom so you may not stay together forever. Now's the time to lay firm foundations for the future.
Taurus Fiery but solid, like a copper beech! You struggle between independence and stability. Could have been engineer, scientist or architect. Looks like a life of reaction now. Example: GLENDA JACKSON.	Taurus will seem rather dull at times, but is a good anchor for family life. You don't have much in common, but you can now forge links for the future.
Gemini The most restless combination in the Zodiac. Highly manic, without any calm qualities or sense of peace. Born to	Lots in common. Arguments a-plenty, which you should both enjoy. Definitely the life to generate sparks between each other.

Sun-Sign   Your own Character   Relating to Others

communicate. Example:
JUDY GARLAND.

Cancer An adventurous
soul with an underlying
homeliness. A good
mixture, and you should
be popular with all sorts
of people – thanks to
kindliness in the past.
Example: GERALD FORD.

Cancer the home-lover, you
the adventurer at heart. I
think you have much to
contribute to each other.

Leo Immensely pleased
with yourself, happy on
the whole but suddenly
gloomy when things go
wrong. Essentially a
giver, not a taker.
Example: PETER
O'TOOLE.

Both enjoy excitement,
glamour, fun. You can feel
great rapport, the result of
good times in the past.

Virgo Free and adaptable
by nature, with an
underlying idealism. A
rover, with few home
ties. In the past you've
been a traveller with a
message to spread.
Example: SIR JOHN
BETJEMAN.

You can understand each
other, even though you're
very different. In the end
you may not like each other
– but are tolerant!

Libra The charming
extrovert, stronger than
most Librans. Almost
certainly a diplomat,
negotiator, leader of
fashion in the past.

A splendid mix. Both of you
have a sense of decency and
fair play. No problems here.

Sun-Sign   Your own Character   Relating to Others

Example: CHARLTON HESTON.

Scorpio Fire and brimstone here. An ardent psyche allied to a determined spirit. Tend to burn your way through life. Could have been in the Inquisition! Example: BILLY GRAHAM.

You don't really respond to Scorpio, so you may deal with each other - without much affection. In this life you're poles apart.

Sagittarius The dedicated traveller, intellectual, philosopher. The ardent preacher, playboy, nature-lover, now and in the past. Example: THE AGA KHAN.

A loose-limbed free-'n'-easy relationship. You do suit each other so well - now and in previous lives.

Capricorn The fun-loving businessman who works hard, plays hard! Have exercised much responsibility in the past, and will do so now. Example: MARY TYLER MOORE.

Capricorn likes to know where he stands, you love the spice of surprise. Not natural friends, but can develop a taste for each other now.

Aquarius The most free-thinking combination in the Zodiac: radical, independent, hating routine. Made to stir up people. Could have been revolutionary in the past. Example: YOKO LENNON.

Great compatibility here. You share an optimistic outlook on life, and can do wonderful creative work together.

Sun-Sign	*Your own Character*	*Relating to Others*
Pisces	Courage mixed with sensitivity. You have tried your hand at many things in the past, and *can* cheat your way through life. Do please strive to settle down! Example: ANDRÉ COURREGES.	Lots of sweetness and understanding, but you can bully each other. Be careful – the wrong behaviour now leads to unhappiness and restriction later.

Psyche in Capricorn: Moon 270 – 299

Your Emotional Nature

From an early age you have built a wall around your heart, out of a need for emotional security. At the beginning, this wall has a definite use, protecting your vulnerable psyche from real – or imagined – onslaughts; but in time it can imprison you, making you too solitary for your own good. Your great aim in life should be to diminish the size of this wall as much as you dare.

It can take many forms. Sometimes it protects you with a veneer of snobbery, encouraging you not to deal with people 'beneath you'. Sometimes it can be a wall of cynicism, protecting you from the need for true and sincere feelings. Sometimes it can be a wall of coldness or inhibition, stopping you from mixing as easily as you should.

At all events, as you know in your heart, you can be a hypocrite, a Scrooge, a fearfully shy person and a scoffer, all because of this Moon-in-Capricorn wall.

At best, however, you have an emotional strength, an ability to survive setbacks, a determination to get to the bones of a situation, that give you definite advantages over your fellow-humans.

Your Folk Memory

Of all the Zodiacal psyches, yours can become most deeply immersed in material reality, to the exclusion of anything else. You can lose touch with your higher self, your soul, your own psychic powers, eventually believing that life is composed of nothing but facts, worldly considerations, and the five senses.

But this descent into worldliness need not be total. At best, you can have the vision of the hermit, seeing much but saying little. Through your dreams and meditations you are most likely to gain *knowledge* rather than emotional excitement, to see the *structure* of spiritual evolution more than its decorative incidentals. Many Moon-in-Capricorn people find it hard to visualize at all. Their dreams are symbolic, perhaps, or a jumble of geometric shapes – not literal visions of the past or anything else.

The part of the Folk Memory to which you are most strongly drawn is the need for emotional and material security. A persistent image could be the ancestral farmer surrounded by family and livestock, surviving a fierce winter; or a town under siege, or an individual suffering privation for a good cause. Your hero is the man of principle, the father-figure, the puritan enduring hardship for the sake of a greater good.

Your nightmares could involve loss of dignity and honour, scenes of dirt and degradation, and, on some bad nights, terrible pangs of guilt stemming straight from your Unconscious.

Links with the Past

A number of past lives have been spent in the pursuit of wealth, power and prestige. You have been concentrating on practical problems, learning how to cope with difficulties, possibly finding out how to survive on your own.

That is one scenario, anyway. The other – if you're now leading a life of reaction – is that you are suddenly experiencing the kind of limitations that you imposed on other people in the past. Probably you are enjoying

– or suffering – a combination of the two.

It is possible, therefore, that as you pass through the turnstiles of a stately home you will see yourself, in a former incarnation, staring haughtily down from a picture-frame – but remember that your inner desire for grandeur will try to convince you of this, whether or not it's true! You could equally have been a stern coal-miner, a Victorian paterfamilias or a military man. Whenever your circumstances, it's likely that you were a man, not a woman.

Your Moon-in-Capricorn feeling for the past could well bring you into touch with the artefacts of a previous existence: the chair, now an antique, that you sat in, the diary that you wrote, the house that you inhabited. And you may be drawn to the country with which you have had dealings in a former incarnation. Those associated with Capricorn are India, Greece and Mexico. I feel the Jewish people have a great link with Capricorn as well, and so memories of life as a Jew could well have the ring of truth.

Links with Spirit

As already explained, you are not someone who can mix easily with other people; but once a friendship is made, it can last a lifetime (or more). In the right-hand column you can see how you relate to people from various Zodiac signs. In the left-hand column you can see the virtues and faults of your own character, depending on your own Sun-sign, with a Moon-in-Capricorn celebrity as an example.

Sun-Sign	Your own Character	Relating to Others
Aries	Rigid inner ideas put across with fire and verve. Powerful personality who may get too big for your boots. Could come a cropper	You make a formidable team in business, but in love you can be too harsh with each other. You have certainly crossed swords in the past.

Sun-Sign	Your own Character	Relating to Others

through the wrong use of power. Beware of wreaking vengeance on people who have hurt you before. Example: IAN PAISLEY.

Taurus Tough, worldly-wise, both a pleasure-lover and a puritan. May be too immersed in this world for your own good. Example: JEREMY THORPE.

Admirable, strong, solid combination. Have come together once again to reinforce lessons partially learnt in the past.

Gemini Schizoid mixture of old man and little boy. Could have been architect, draughtsman, teacher in past. Clearly you are making a break with your recent development. Example: CHARLES AZNAVOUR.

Meant to be poles apart, but actually you get on well – provided you complement not fight each other. At worst you are paying each other back for past wrongs.

Cancer Deeply conservative type living in the past. Have absorbed many stable values, and are now radiating them to the world. Example: 'Poldark' author WINSTON GRAHAM.

You suit each other well: ideal for family life. Whatever your sex, you play father to Cancer – perhaps as you did in the past.

Sun-Sign Your own Character	*Relating to Others*
Leo Figure of power, shrewd but childlike in some ways. Stubborn pride is your worst fault, honour your greatest virtue. Greatest need: to unclench your soul. Example: ARCHBISHOP MAKARIOS.	It's easy for this combination to become a battle for dominance. You have been trained in different ways of exercising power – so can easily clash now.
Virgo Self-contained creature, tending to live in the past. You have been worldly yet spiritual: a political priest, perhaps, an ascetic businessman. Example: YVONNE DE CARLO.	Together you can form a stable, long-term partnership – very much a repeat of earlier relationships.
Libra Soft on the outside, tough inside. If a woman, probably just changed over from being a man. You are being taught in this life how to temper justice with mercy. Example: JOAN FONTAINE.	It's tempting for you to push Libra around. In the past you have won the battle for dominance, so now you must yield power for the sake of love.
Scorpio Tough, no-nonsense character probably coming to a full stop in this life. You face experiences that bring you face to face with your own nature. Example: SPIRO AGNEW.	You can be ineluctably drawn together – by your own karma. What both of you must learn is how to bind up your wounds with love – and start anew.

Sun-Sign	*Your own Character*	*Relating to Others*

Sagittarius An uneasy mixture of sternness and laughter – great if you can integrate them together. You have been a preacher, politician or army commander before. Example: MATT MONRO.

You can get on well, so long as you enjoy Sagittarius's free-'n'-easy ways. You are being encouraged to follow Sagittarius's lead in this life.

Capricorn At best, the most reliable and straightforward person. At worst, someone trapped in materialism, like a pot-holer coming to a dead-end. Example: Moors murderer IAN BRADY.

Obviously there can be good rapport here, with a solid emotional understanding. A cold and dry relationship that needs more warmth and colour in this life.

Aquarius An up-tight heart in a wide-open spirit. A chance for a caged bird to fly free again. Example: MIA FARROW.

Good rapport, but a terribly cool relationship. You're being shown a new direction by Aquarius.

Pisces Intriguing mixture of good practical sense and artistic idealism. Key Life could have been in a monastery. This may be the life when you learn what sacrifice means. Example: film-maker ROBERT ALTMAN.

You can be too hard and canny for Pisces, but with this relationship you can learn to be more generous and loving.

Psyche in Aquarius: Moon 300 – 329

Your Emotional Nature

The Aquarian psyche is the most difficult to describe in all the Zodiac. In one way your emotional demeanour is strong and determined; in another, curiously dispassionate. You can be reasonable one moment, and utterly unpredictable the next. Proud, yet quite unsnobbish. Logical, yet given to sudden intuitions.

Nobody quite knows what reaction to expect from you – least of all yourself, at times! In some ways you are extremely careful in your judgments, but equally you can make hasty decisions apparently on the spur of the moment. Where people in general are concerned, you can be unfeeling at times; you can make sweeping statements about nations or social groups that have a definite note of inhumanity. But when it comes to individual people you are much more caring, defending personal rights and freedoms above everything.

Your response to life is lively and observant, but not particularly sensual. You are capable of being equally friendly to both men and woman – indeed, you don't seem to notice their sexuality in your dealings with them. It's as though you're above such worldly attitudes!

Your Folk Memory

Your kind of clairvoyance is not based on feelings but on mental images: claircognizance, it could be called. At special moments you can see the *idea* behind a series of events, the *point* being made by your life's experiences. You can also get premonitions of future events, though again more in symbols than literal detail.

The part of the Folk Memory to which you're tuned is the great step forward: the moments of decisive advance when mankind enters a new era of development. You may recall the episodes in the film *2001* when the ape-man discovered the use of weapons or when the astronauts ventured into deep space.

On each occasion a strange black obelisk appeared. It represented Aquarius, the sign of the future.

The typical hero of a Moon-in-Aquarius dream or meditation is a spaceman from another planet: the stranger who knows more than the natives. This hero can take the form of the scientist surrounded by dunces, a woman of startling intelligence, even an animal with uncanny powers. If a unicorn ever appears in your dreams, it's a sure sign that you are directly in touch with the deepest layers of your psyche.

Other favourite images will be a bird, a rainbow and miracles, especially the gift of changing people's minds through your own telepathy. If your psyche is at ease, you will adore flying in your dreams, swooping without fear; but if you are inwardly ill-at-ease, you will be unable to fly – or may start falling in mid-air.

Links with the Past

In recent lives your soul has been developing along Aquarian lines: learning both how to be independent and, contrariwise, how to be part of a group.

This could have involved experiences as a radical thinker, one of a revolutionary party, a member of a scientific team or one of the many groups of people who chose – or were forced – to adopt an entirely new lifestyle.

Aquarius is very much linked with the settlement of America and the founding of the Union, so you could have been one of the Pilgrim Fathers. It's also associated with the French Revolution, and indeed you could have been involved in any one of the many European movements for justice and human rights in the past 200 years. In England, you could have been a Quaker, a Leveller, a Roundhead or an early trades unionist.

Most of all, Aquarius is identified with the Communist and Anarchist movements of the past 100 years. However it may offend your political sentiments now, you may well have been swayed by workers' power in a recent life in Europe or Russia.

In all these social movements one's sexuality was not important. So it's quite possible that in a recent life you were an early champion of women's rights.

In your experiences as a free-thinker, you will have trodden on a number of toes, so there may well be a karmic legacy to come to terms with now. You may be forced to accept social conditions that do not give you the freedom you desire. More probably, you may have a child whose desire for independence seems like a rejection of yourself.

Links with Spirit

I've indicated that you can mix freely with all kinds of people, even though you are an independent type who needs personal freedom. In the right-hand column below, you can see how you relate to people from various Zodiac signs. In the left-hand column you can see how your Moon-in-Aquarius virtues and faults merge with those of your Sun-sign spirit. Also indicated is a celebrity sharing the same combination.

Sun-Sign Your own Character	*Relating to Others*
Aries Utterly free and independent spirit, attracted to whatever is new and experimental. A prophet, inventor, radical thinker. Example: PETER BROOK.	A happy link here, for you both know the value of personal freedom. A new start for both of you in this life.
Taurus A spirit caught between past and future, emotionally free-ranging but still tied to old attitudes. Your need is to produce something	Not an easy link at times, for you find Taurus too dull and stolid. Your job is to give Taurus a push in a new direction.

Sun-Sign   Your own Character   Relating to Others

practical out of your
bright ideas. Example:
ORSON WELLES.

Gemini A born rebel, full
of charm and talent but
impossibly frisky and
restless at times. A circus
juggler, metaphorically
(and perhaps literally)
now and in the past.
Example: GEORGE BEST.

Excellent links. Almost
certainly you have worked
together fruitfully in the
past. Now you can renew
the friendship without any
hang-ups.

Cancer Striking talent in
one direction, but very
moody and emotional,
which can spoil the
overall effect. Security
and peace are what your
spirit is trying to absorb.
Example: VIVIEN
MERCHANT.

Emotionally you will find
Cancer too cloying for your
taste. You are being
mothered by Cancer, and
you don't always like it!

Leo A spry, warm and
humane soul trying to be
prince and democrat at
the same time Great gifts
of the spirit here.
Example: JOHN HUSTON.

Can be lovely links so long
as you don't allow pride to
obstruct the flow of love.

Virgo A cool personality,
rather clever and
ingenious. Could have
been a book-keeper in the
past. In this life you are
being forced to specialize.
Example: DENIS HEALEY.

Good mental links, but at
heart you may find Virgo a
bit critical and narrow-
minded. It's your job to
wake Virgo up, and give the
relationship some pep.

Sun-Sign	Your own Character	Relating to Others

Libra A lovely combination of intelligence and charm. Your greatest difficulty is joining in instead of staying on the sidelines. Example: ARTHUR MILLER.

Excellent links here; there should be a wonderful flow of mental rapport between you – the result of much practice in the past.

Scorpio Sharp, immensely proud, very free and also very possessive and jealous. Lots of karma to be worked out as a result of a wrong direction in the past. Example: VIVIEN LEIGH.

Not an easy combination, as Scorpio wants to intensify where you want to relax and make easy. You may get drawn into this relationship against your better judgment.

Sagittarius Another free-as-air, speculative personality wanting to explore ideas, places, people. You can't be tied down. Example: WOODY ALLEN.

Brilliantly successful links between you. Could well have been scientists together. A chance now to develop along similar lines in this life.

Capricorn A psyche that floats like a butterfly, a spirit that stings like a bee! In the past you have been a revolutionary; now is the time to be serious and steady. Example: MUHAMMED ALI.

Quite good links, though you will be infuriated by Capricorn's constant realism and dignity. You are both learning the same lesson, from different ends of the spectrum.

Aquarius The pure egghead mentality, ultra-cool and observant,

Obviously a perfect match though a platonic rather than sensual union. You can

Sun-Sign	*Your own Character*	*Relating to Others*
	humane and reasonable. This could be a Key Life for many lives to come. Example: FRANÇOIS TRUFFAUT.	develop your brains as a group mentality.
Pisces	Icy but yielding, intelligence in the service of mankind. You have been an artist, designer or great beauty in your time. Example: URSULA ANDRESS.	Both of you are idealistic, but you will find Pisces a bit emotional at times.

Psyche in Pisces: Moon 330 – 359

Your Emotional Nature

As you know full well, your emotional disposition is soft, tender and oh, so vulnerable! Whatever your outward temperament may be, inwardly you are a creature of deep, rich, fluctuating feelings.

You find it hard to respond to life with any great consistency. Instead, you react to events immediately around you, without seeing them in a proper perspective. Sometimes you respond out of fear or anger, but usually out of sentiment. As soon as you see someone in distress, you want to help. Your psyche is wildly charitable.

It's difficult for you to adopt a strong, positive attitude of dominance over others. Your natural attitude, *vis-à-vis* others, is a position of friendly submission, going along with their plans and desires, adapting yourself to their needs rather than the other way round.

Your emotional nature thrives on kindness, gentility and sweet human love. If conditions get too harsh, your impulse is to run off – to escape into a world of make-believe. You have a highly active imagination which sometimes works to your advantage, but often misleads you by exaggerating your heart-felt emotions at the expense of your commonsense.

Your Folk Memory

You have the most psychic psyche imaginable! For most of your waking and certainly sleeping hours, you are closely in touch with your own Unconscious and, indeed, with our Collective Unconscious. A constant stream of feelings and intuitions flow from them into your everyday consciousness. More than any other Zodiacal representative, you are a creature of unseen worlds.

The part of our Folk Memory that most appeals to you is the need for escape. This can take the form of sleep itself, the telling of stories, the venturing into fantasy, and, more generally, the etheric quality of life – the way that many worlds interpenetrate our own.

For this reason, you may not have a good psychic memory for precise visual details such as places and faces you have known in the past, but you have a wonderful capacity for recalling the emotional flavour of old experiences – how you *felt* at the time. In other words, you may not ever see the flames licking at the stake, but you could still recall the *pain* of a medieval death.

Typically happy dreams will involve merging, yielding and slipping away: the path of a fish, in fact, gliding through submarine depths. Any image that defies gravity, fuzzes an outline or brings separate elements blissfully together would be typical of your dream-life. Nightmares, on the other hand, could involve vertigo, loss of identity, fear of wild beasts – any situation, in fact, where you feel out of your natural element.

Links with the Past

With your Piscean psyche you have clearly spent a number of
recent lives learning to be sensitive and frail. This could have
been through apparently accidental circumstances – such as
loss of family and friends, or separation through war – but it
could have been a matter of choice, such as entering holy
orders.

If you feel your present incarnation is a life of reaction, you
have probably returned quite quickly. You could have been a
combatant in the First World War who has come back fast to
know what it's like to be at the receiving end of harsh
conditions. If, on the other hand, you feel this is a life of
continuity, your Key Life could have been a long time ago,
when spiritual values were more treasured than they are
nowadays.

Countries linked with Pisces are Portugal, the Polynesian
Islands, and parts of North Africa bordering on the Sahara.
You may have spent a life or two in one of these places.

Less happily, Pisces is also linked with the escapist use of
drink and drugs. Thus you may have had difficult experiences
in the past to do with alcohol and other narcotics, and your
reaction to them today will indicate whether you conquered
these addictions or are still tempted by them.

Links with Spirit

You want to meet people, so long as they are friendly and
approachable, so in the left-hand column you can see the
virtues and faults of your total character, depending on your
own Sun-sign, with a Moon-in-Pisces celebrity as an example.

Sun-Sign Your own Character	*Relating to Others*
Aries Inwardly sensitive, outwardly dynamic. You are being taught the	You can get hurt by Aries, but can teach humanity and gentleness. Not a sensible

Sun-Sign   Your own Character   Relating to Others

danger of sadism and masochism at the same time! You must steer the middle path as best you may. Example: ANDRE PREVIN.

mix, but good can come out of it.

Taurus Intriguing character, half-elf and half-gnome! Level-headed one moment, naive and sentimental the next. After a period of floating, you are now coming down to earth. Example: AUDREY HEPBURN.

At a spiritual level, you have much to contribute to each other's development; at a day-to-day level, you are hopelessly different.

Gemini Nervy, clever, soulful – you have had a fascinatingly diverse range of experience. You are trying to marry heart and head together. Example: VIRGINIA McKENNA.

You seem magnificently well matched in public – but in private you'll have many tensions. Tolerance is the great virtue to develop.

Cancer Richly emotional personality, able to flow into other people's hearts. Very feminine in outlook, whatever your actual sex. Could spend your life running away from your real identity. Example: SUSAN HAYWARD.

Wonderful rapport possible, though you may be too emotional for each other. In past lives you were clearly entwined, and now you have karma together.

Sun-Sign   Your own Character   Relating to Others

Leo Imaginative yet arrogant, highly intuitive, rather a 'grand opera' sort of person. Easy for your sense of power to get overbearing. Example: ROBERT BOLT.

Lovely so long as you are children together. If you have to grow up, there will be signs of immaturity.

Virgo Highly sensitive, fussy, idealistic and out-of-this-world person. Clearly a monk or mystic in previous lives. Example: CHRISTOPHER ISHERWOOD.

Good links for a rather special, idealistic relationship though you can certainly get on each other's nerves at a day-to-day level.

Libra Soft and charming, rather weak at times, apt to be the victim of other people. Could be a life of reaction, to show you what it's like to be hurt. Example: RITA HAYWORTH.

Ideal sort of relationship since you make so few demands on each other. Possibly you have been hurt by others, and you are comforting each other in this life.

Scorpio Sensitive but with great inner strength. Escapist in one way, highly responsible in another. Probably a dancer, singer, priest or poet in a previous life. Example: PRINCESS GRACE OF MONACO.

Good links, so long as you don't allow Scorpio to bully you. Very psychic together, but you can't either of you forgive and forget easily.

Sagittarius Fluent and

Good links, but you both

Sun-Sign   Your own Character   Relating to Others

easy, frisky and restless. You are moving fast through a variety of experiences in this and recent lives, but do not absorb all the lessons quickly enough. Example: FRANK SINATRA.

are restless and may not have the stamina to stay together. The sea could be a link from the past that is symbolic of your relationship.

Capricorn So soft and escapist in one way, such a tough person in another. There could be an air of melancholy, as though denied something you desire most of all. Example: MARLENE DIETRICH.

Not an easy relationship. A bad experience in a past life could spell trouble this time around. Beware of finding Capricorn too cold.

Aquarius Clever but easily swayed. Very susceptible, especially to experiences denied to you in any earlier life. Probably a musician or writer last time round. Example: NED SHERRIN.

Quite good links here. One of your tasks in life is to teach Aquarius how to make a steady emotional commitment – not easy!

Pisces A mass of nerves, easy-going to the point of ditheriness. Your big test is how to stay sensitive and sensible at the same time. Example: DAVID NIVEN.

Obviously you have strong ties. You have the responsibility of showing Pisces how to find emotional peace.

CHAPTER NINE

Masks and Costumes

In Chapter Six, FIGURING IT OUT, you were shown how to calculate the House positions of the Sun and Moon. These, very broadly, give a clue to your *karma* and *dharma* – that is, the debts that you have brought from the past and the duties and opportunities that confront you in the present.

In just the same way that an actor wears make-up and costume to describe the character he is playing, so do we wear different disguises provided by the Sun and Moon. In Chapters Seven and Eight, you saw the real nature of your SPIRIT and PSYCHE at the moment. But these House positions tell you something extra. Just as an actor's make-up, with its lines and wrinkles, tells us what life has done to this character in the past, so do the Node House positions tell you what your Key Life has done to you in an earlier incarnation. In the same way, an actor's costume shows what the character thinks of himself now and where he thinks he's going in his life today; and your East House positions tell you where your present life is taking you.

Broadly speaking, the NODE HOUSES refer to the past, while the EAST HOUSES refer to the present.

Once again, I must ask you to take my remarks merely as suggestions, hopefully setting your own inner imagination in motion. To help you, I've given numerous examples of famous people born under each category. Take these as interesting, perhaps extra-special illustrations of what each House position means – but don't assume that, because you share an astrological factor with Jimmy Carter, you will necessarily become President of the United States! The same people turn up more than once, so that you can see how past and present lives interweave with each other.

SUN IN THE HOUSES

Sun in 1ST NODE House In the past you've been a vivid and personable individual, an extrovert with a great desire to impress the world with your cleverness, charm and charisma. You were given the opportunity to glow – and according to the Sun's East House position, you can judge how well you acquitted yourself. If the Sun lies in the 1st, 7th or 10th East House, you did well – like, for instance, the cellist PAUL TORTELLIER or the actor ALEC GUINNESS. Another celebrity with Sun in this 1st Node House was NELSON ROCKEFELLER.

Sun in 1ST EAST House Clearly your task in this life is positive and forward-looking. Your inner duty is to project your personality in a clear-cut, dominant way. You may well be a pioneer in your work, or a leader among your circle of friends. To have the Sun in this position suggests that your life will be a Key Life for several incarnations to come. It could well be a second-breath life or else the climax to a series of lives of continuity. Obviously this is a much-frequented House position for celebrities in all walks of life. These include LAURENCE OLIVIER, MAE WEST, President LYNDON JOHNSON and impressionist MIKE YARWOOD.

Sun in 2ND NODE House You could have been active in business or the arts in your Key Life. You were a determined person, either in a life of reaction or continuity, with a warm and generous heart. If you have a stubborn streak in this life, it's almost certainly a hangover from the past. Any creative talent will also have come from this previous life – as, for example, in the case of WALT DISNEY. Other celebrities who were probably in business in earlier lives are HAROLD WILSON and JOHN LINDSAY, both now in politics, and JEAN-PAUL BELMONDO.

Sun in 2ND EAST House Your great task in life is to root yourself in reality. You have a fine business head, a feeling for property and antiques, and you can help your fellow-men in solid, practical ways. You must learn how to be patient – and should try to restrain your own pride, which can be fearsome. Best example is the man who pulled France together, more than once: CHARLES DE GAULLE.

Sun in 3RD NODE House You led a versatile and interesting life before this one – either as a writer and lecturer (ENOCH POWELL), a salesman or trader (LYNDON JOHNSON), a tutor (ROGER WHITTAKER) or head of a large commercial enterprise (MARGARET THATCHER). You were probably quick-witted and popular, and a brother or sister in that life could play an important role in your life today (JACQUELINE KENNEDY ONASSIS). Any skills as a communicator that you have in this life have certainly come straight from this previous Key Life. Probably a life of continuity.

Sun in 3RD EAST House Without doubt, your talent in this life is in the use or words, spoken and written. You may be a writer (LAWRENCE DURRELL), a speechmaker (SIR WINSTON CHURCHILL), an actress (BETTE DAVIS) or simply the most charming loudmouth of them all (MUHAMMED ALI)! You are betraying your duty if you fail to spread the word, if you keep quiet when you should speak the truth, or if you misuse your gifts in an unworthy way.

Sun in 4TH NODE House In your Key Life you were a traditionist absorbing the lessons of the past. You may have been a gentle mothering type like GERALD FORD (clearly in a life of continuity). You may have been defending a particular culture from disappearing (like KING HUSSEIN OF JORDAN). Or you may have been imprisoned in a dead, over-protective society, from which (like FIDEL CASTRO) you are now escaping. This Key Life will give you a sense of lasting values, and still make it possible for you to care for and protect people around you.

Sun in 4TH EAST House Your duty is to preserve the past (like BARBARA CARTLAND) and maintain a conservative set of values (like EDWARD HEATH or HAROLD MACMILLAN) – but, as these two politicians have shown, this does not necessarily mean stuck in the past. It's a constantly renewing process, merging the old with the new. The great conductor HERBERT VON KARAJAN has reinterpreted the music of Beethoven (with whom he may have been closely associated in the past), while GEORGE HARRISON is bringing through memories of earlier musical training (especially lives spent in India).

Sun in 5TH NODE House Your last life will have been a creative, lively one, much devoted to love, pleasure and recreation. You could have been an entertainer (like MUHAMMED ALI) or a politician who gained power through charisma or inheritance rather than pure talent (many examples, including JOHN and ROBERT KENNEDY, ANTHONY EDEN and JO GRIMOND). Any of these could have been aristocrats or even royalty, for this House is closely linked with noble families: for instance, PRINCESS MARGARET and PRINCESS ANNE were probably royal in their previous lives as well.

Sun in 5TH EAST House This is a life when you feel you are born to deserve power and prestige – like PRINCE PHILIP, PRINCE CHARLES and PRINCESS MARGARET. You have lots of good humour, energy and the desire to impress others. Beware of getting too arrogant, though. It isn't easy to feel and act like a king in a democratic society – as RICHARD NIXON has found to his cost. He is probably leading a dead-end life, but you may well be enjoying a second-breath life. The danger with too many 5th House lives of continuity is that you get too cocky and out of touch.

Sun in 6TH NODE House Your Key Life was probably spent in a low-key capacity: as servant, clerk, academic or power behind the throne. (Lovely thought: was CHARLES DE GAULLE once Cardinal Richelieu?) I can see astronomer PATRICK MOORE as an intellectual hermit now getting the chance to burst into public notoriety. DAVID FROST, too, may have been a very quiet mouse indeed: perhaps a humble secretary to some great statesman. PETER USTINOV could have been a craftsman, translator or Figaro-like figure. All these examples suggest that people with this Sun-position can jump out of nowhere and lead successful lives next time round.

Sun in 6TH EAST House You see your life in terms of service to others. You have quite a humble approach to life, and a good grasp of detail (for instance, pioneer animator WALT DISNEY). Two politicians exemplify the quiet, modest approach of the 6th House type: Presidents GERALD FORD and FRANKLIN ROOSEVELT. This is a life where personal desires must be set to one side. On the face of it, ADOLF HITLER seems the complete opposite; but he saw himself as an instrument of destiny, a servant of the Aryan race. But be warned: if you get too fussy and critical, you can seem a little Fuehrer at times!

Sun in 7TH NODE House Your Key Life will have been an artistic one, or you could have been a woman. Unlikely as it may seem, ERNEST HEMINGWAY and JAMES DEAN were leading lives of reaction against this soft, feminine quality in their souls. More understandably, both PRINCE CHARLES and

GEORGE HARRISON could have been women, too, in earlier lives. The same applies to politician WILLIAM WHITELAW. You will have been a sensitive, perhaps vulnerable individual, and there will be a great temptation in your present life to pay people back for wrongs they did to you earlier.

Sun in 7TH EAST House A pleasant, lovable personality. Certainly your aim in this life should be to spread peace and contentment. You may well come into contact with people whom you have wronged in the past; now you must wash this karma away with conciliation and affection. Two great charmers of the screen had the Sun in this position: CHARLES BOYER and the passionate collector of paintings, EDWARD G. ROBINSON.

Sun in 8TH NODE House Probably you had a difficult and testing Key Life, which your present life is trying to assuage. You may have been in great danger, or you may have faced considerable injustice: SIR WINSTON CHURCHILL, for instance. You may have been cruel and unfeeling, so that, like DAVID BOWIE and possibly MIA FARROW, you have come back to face some of the people whom you may have hurt in the past. There could have been a history of sexual hang-ups and excesses; and perhaps the romantic BARBARA CARTLAND is making amends for an orgiastic past!

Sun in 8TH EAST House Anyone with the Sun in this position is liable to face real hardship, sacrifice and disappointment: a kind of crucifixion that perhaps fixes your present life as a dead-end life or a hard life of reaction. It's fascinating, for instance, that the assassinated JOHN KENNEDY, and his wife JACKIE and murdered brother ROBERT, all had the Sun in this position. So did HELEN KELLER, battling against great physical misfortunes. And so, more brutishly, did the mass murderer CHARLES MANSON. Within your heart, you may feel strongly pulled by fate in one particular direction.

Sun in 9TH NODE House Your last life will have been an adventurous and exciting time, with your soul opening up new experiences. You may have been a constant traveller (like RINGO STARR) or diplomat (like HENRY CABOT LODGE), or scholar (like RICHARD ROGERS) or publisher and *bon viveur* (like MIKE YARWOOD). It could have been a second-breath life, or, if you're a Sagittarian now, you could be in a series of lives of continuity. The karma you have collected could involve indiscretion, carelessness and a wayward way with the opposite sex.

Sun in 9TH EAST House This should be a relatively agreeable and public-spirited lifetime for you. Your soul is in a positive and extrovert mood, and you yearn to expand the scope of your projects, travel as much as possible, and give to life as generously as you take. Two politicians, very similar in outlook, were NELSON ROCKEFELLER and JO GRIMOND, while another statesman, less moderate in his 9th House exuberance, was BENITO MUSSOLINI.

Sun in 10TH NODE House Here's an indication that your previous Key Life was a powerful and important one. You won't necessarily have been a celebrity known to history, but you could well have been a manufacturer, politician, governor or head of some organization. It's hard to resist the thought that QUEEN ELIZABETH II was a monarch in her previous life. So, possibly, was RICHARD NIXON (he still thinks he is one!). Was BETTE DAVIS a slave-driver? Were you? If you did not exercise responsibility properly in those days, the tables may now be turned on you with a vengeance.

Sun in 10TH EAST House This is a life of great opportunity: the chance to bring to culmination a long effort of training in the past. You should be able to manipulate people quite well, put practical schemes into effect, and command a good deal of attention. The danger is that, instead of fulfilling good dharma, you will waste your chances and earn bad karma for next time round. Celebrities who are leading this kind of life are HAROLD WILSON, DAVID FROST and PRINCESS ANNE.

Sun in 11TH NODE House In your Key Life you will have been a radical figure, ahead of your time, perhaps good at science, languages and philosophy. You could have been a teacher, scholar, man of affairs, high-spirited woman or social reformer. Can you see LAURENCE OLIVIER as an influential lady associated with affairs of state? Or HAROLD MACMILLAN as one of the American Founding Fathers? or HARRY SECOMBE, believe it or not, running a charitable institution and exerting a great influence for good in his time?

Sun in 11TH EAST House There are three obvious paths open to you. You could, like WERNER VON BRAUN, devote yourself to the scientific future, in however small a capacity. Or you could, like ANTHONY EDEN and VALERY GISCARD D'ESTAING, be on the disciplined, fair-minded wing of politics? Or, if you were very talented, you could be a kind of roving internationalist like PETER USTINOV, turning your amiable mind to a variety of pleasant, not very taxing problems. A forward-looking life – but make sure that you don't spend it always sitting on the fence.

Sun in 12TH NODE House Your previous life was a quiet affair, perhaps in a religious setting. Less happily, you could have been an escapist, running away from responsibilities. It's easy to put BILLY GRAHAM and BENJAMIN BRITTEN into clerical garb, and perhaps MICK JAGGER and GRACIE FIELDS into more poetic clothes. It may well have been a life of sacrifice in some way. I can see KEVIN KEEGAN as a cripple who has now earned the right to marvellous physical mobility. For some of you, there could be a psychic gift, a legacy coming straight from this earlier life.

Sun in 12TH EAST House Not many people in this bustling age will be enjoying a life of continuity here. One was GRACIE FIELDS, clearly relishing the same talent that she'd had before. Probably suffering a dead-end life has been the DUCHESS OF WINDSOR, taking escapism to its depressing conclusion. For this 12th House makes you fey, sensitive, in tune with your soul, inclined to suffer injustice at some stage in your life, and a dreamer – sometimes, as in the case of MARGARET THATCHER, a determined woman of vision.

MOON IN THE HOUSES

Moon in 1ST NODE House Your role as a mother will have been important in the past – perhaps literally, in the case of QUEEN ELIZABETH II. But this motherliness could have taken the form of a protective, caring attitude – towards people in your charge, a property that you loved, a desire to help the world around you. DAVID FROST, in his previous life, could have been the solicitous servant to a much admired master. HAROLD MACMILLAN, as an 18th-century American statesman, could have 'mothered' his people through the birth of their independent nation.

Moon in 1ST EAST House You have an emotional attitude to life, though this may be kept under control by other factors. There's something of the actor about you. You like to feel that you are helping other people – but when things go wrong, you tend to become a bit hysterical. You are likely to have deep roots in your own family or the place where you were born – witness the identification of HARRY SECOMBE with Wales,

HAROLD WILSON with Yorkshire, and LYNDON JOHNSON with Texas.

Moon in 2ND NODE House In your Key Life you will have been immersed in a particular family, country or background, so that it seeped deeply into your soul. Who can doubt, for instance, that LAWRENCE DURRELL spent his Key Life around the Mediterranean? And surely BARBARA CARTLAND must have been a Regency belle (or a buck)? You will have had an exaggerated regard for *things* – either for their monetary or aesthetic value. You will also have enjoyed the sensual side of life. If, in your present life, you have a delicate appetite for food or sex, you may have over-eaten too generously in the past!

Moon in 2ND EAST House In your present life you are emotionally devoting yourself to the good things in life: the warmth of human love, the pleasures of the earthly appetites. Both MICK JAGGER and PETER USTINOV have the Moon in this position; and both have a similar liking for the comforts of this world. Both, too, have a soft, amiable nature, wanting to be generous to their friends, famous for their hospitality, open with their affections. You should be the same.

Moon in 3RD NODE House In your Key Life you had a varied experience, travelling a good deal, stretching your mind, and mixing with a wide range of people. Emotionally you won't have been very stable; if so, like PRINCESS MARGARET, you could now be suffering a similar instability in the relationships of this life. There are links between this House and the 6th, 9th and 11th Houses. If, like WILLIE WHITELAW, the Moon lies in your 11th East House, for instance, you are clearly in a series of lives of continuity, undergoing the same kind of experiences.

Moon in 3RD EAST House Very much a life where you need to communicate with others. You may be a professional speech-maker like FIDEL CASTRO, a performer like MIA FARROW, or a compulsive talker like MUHAMMED ALI. (Ali also has Sun in 3rd East House – an indication that he has a double-strength gift of the gab!) Your opportunity in life involves the number of friends you can make, the amount of knowledge you can absorb, and the success with which you can cope with frequent changes of pace and mood in your emotional life.

Moon in 4TH NODE House Your Key Life will have been spent in an emotional atmosphere that was close and a bit clannish. I can imagine KING HUSSEIN closeted within an inward-looking Middle Eastern society; or ENOCH POWELL as an Indian maharajah. Either you will have been a woman of powerful feelings yourself, or else under the influence of such a woman. It's interesting that ALEC GUINNESS is a Catholic convert in this life, clearly drawn back to the 'family' that played a big role in his earlier lives.

Moon in 4TH EAST House Emotionally you're a pretty old-fashioned person, however much you pay lip-service to modern ideas. You have a strong feeling for home and family, and you're a natural patriot. WALT DISNEY, although inventing a new art-form, created stories that were sentimental and family-oriented. ANTHONY EDEN was a high Tory, with a romantic view of Britain's place in the world. Interestingly, the DUCHESS OF WINDSOR has the Moon in this position. Is she, I wonder, a karmic black sheep yearning to return to her true family?

Moon in 5TH NODE House Your Key Life had quite a jolly, extrovert emotional atmosphere – possibly with a show-business connection, a well-to-do background, or simply a friendly and affectionate home life. SIR WINSTON CHURCHILL would certainly have had an enjoyable lifestyle, probably in the same family two centuries earlier. HAROLD WILSON, too, will have come from a warm-hearted, pleased-as-Punch background in a previous life. People with Moon in this position are capable of summing up a great inner self-confidence, as though they have a nice cushion of emotional assurance to fall back on.

Moon in 5TH EAST House This gives the inner desire to feel like a king. You want to glow with other people's approval. Emotionally you can be flattered, even if other parts of your soul are not so easily fooled. It is, pre-eminently, an indication of a stage-struck personality – someone who does love to be loved! But with this lovability comes a certain arrogance at times – witness CHARLES DE GAULLE, ENOCH POWELL and JACQUELINE KENNEDY ONASSIS. Remember – with the Moon in this position, your emotional duty is to *give* rather than take.

Moon in 6TH NODE House This suggests that your Key Life had a slightly secluded lifestyle. Emotionally you may have felt cramped by a particular dogma, or your relationships may not have been as fulfilling as you'd have liked. Your health, too, may have suffered. I think it's possible to see PRINCESS ANNE as a straitlaced lady, inhibited by circumstances rather than by any natural coldness. EDWARD KENNEDY, too, could have been a much cooler, subfusc person in his last life than he appears today. And perhaps the larger-than-life MUHAMMED ALI is over-compensating now for the deprivations and emotional disabilities he was forced to suffer earlier.

Moon in 6TH EAST House I think it's possible to see that, emotionally, there's a common factor running through all people with Moon in this position. Inwardly, it encourages a cool, neat, controlled and self-aware emotional nature that cannot easily throw caution to the winds. Such people range from ELIZABETH II, RICHARD NIXON and VALERY GISCARD D'ESTAING to DAVID FROST and HAROLD MACMILLAN.

Moon in 7TH NODE House You are a person with a loving and generous heart in your last life – someone who gave yourself, perhaps foolishly, to one partner or to the world at large. You could have been quite a passive type, allowing this other person to dictate what you should do, say and think. But you will also have had a great emotional skill in reaching compromises. ROBERT KENNEDY was one such person. So were MIA FARROW and GRACIE FIELDS.

Moon in 7TH EAST House Emotionally you have a most affable and relaxed manner, with the ability to get on with a wide variety of people. Sometimes you can be pushed around too easily by people who have an emotional hold over you. This may be a continuation of a past pattern – as in the case of GRACIE FIELDS (see 7th Node Moon above). Certainly the need to find the partner with whom you can be emotionally at peace is paramount; and probably BENJAMIN BRITTEN, through his long-life friendship with Peter Pears, was a good example.

Moon in 8TH NODE House Your last life was emotionally fraught, perhaps leaving a wound on your psyche that is still painful in your present life. Like the DUCHESS OF WINDSOR, you could have rejected people who loved you, with un- fortunate consequences in this life. Or, like ERNEST HEMINGWAY, you could have betrayed the trust that people placed in you – a fault that came back to haunt him in his life this century. Certainly some emotional trauma will have occurred in your Key Life, which you must now wash away, if possible.

Moon in 8TH EAST House At some stage in your life, you may have to experience rejection, disappointment and sacrifice. Someone will let you down, or you will feel bereft of help and comfort. Three famous examples are CHARLES CHAPLIN, unfairly exiled from Hollywood for his political views; EDWARD HEATH, removed from the Tory leadership; and EDWARD KENNEDY, robbed of his brothers' friendship and support. It's an emotional atmosphere that can make you paranoid at times.

Moon in 9TH NODE House Emotionally your last life will have been a high-spirited affair, lively and inquiring and essentially optimistic. It's easy to picture JOHN KENNEDY as a buoyant and enthusiastic figure; CHARLES DE GAULLE as a man of considerable intellect, with a great interest in foreign affairs; and SIMONE DE BEAUVOIR as a preacher. You will have been imbued with something of the same fervent, questioning mood.

Moon in 9TH EAST House Your mood in this life is that of a traveller: eager for variety and new experience. You prefer the new to the old, and you like to take nothing for granted. This is a life when you can widen your emotional range; get to know a larger spectrum of people than in earlier lives; and perhaps start a number of relationships that will figure prominently in lives to come. The best example of this temperament is the impressionist MIKE YARWOOD, whose skill at mimicking people is really his way of expanding his range of human contacts.

Moon in 10TH NODE House With the Moon in this position, you will have spent your Key Life in an atmosphere of power. You will have absorbed a political or business environment, and may well have been a powerful figure yourself; your job may not have been important, but your emotional influence was great. People who fall into this category are EDWARD HEATH, PRINCE PHILIP and ANTHONY EDEN.

Moon in 10TH EAST House This is a life when you must exercise great emotional responsibility. Your feelings must be controlled; you must act in a discreet way; and you will have to be, by turns, tactful, shrewd, cautious and determined, in order to have influence over others. People who are clearly responding positively to this factor are PRINCE CHARLES and MARGARET THATCHER. Someone who has used this force in a wrong way is CHARLES MANSON.

Moon in 11TH NODE House Your Key Life was not a very emotional time for you. Instead, you were developing other sides of your soul, and affairs of the heart were not particularly important to you. In the case of RICHARD NIXON, this influence has continued through into his present life. In the same way, with the DUKE OF WINDSOR the independence of outlook developed in his earlier life continued into his 20th-century incarnation – independence from responsibility.

Moon in 11TH EAST House This encourages you to widen your contacts, meet new people and develop a cool, caring but dispassionate approach to life. Emotionally you are learning – perhaps with difficulty – how to be tolerant, clear-thinking at times of crisis, and diplomatic to everyone, without favouring some and rejecting others. You may see something of this attitude in the lives of PRINCESS ANNE, GERALD FORD and ROGER WHITTAKER.

Moon in 12TH NODE House In your last life you will have had a psychic quality. This may have been temporarily lost in your present incarnation, or may still be there, perhaps incorporated into your overall emotional disposition. JACKIE ONASSIS was clearly a sensitive, vulnerable person in her Key Life – a sensitivity that will have been tested in the searing experiences of her current existence. PRINCE CHARLES, too, will have had some special religious training in the past that is assisting him in his life at the moment.

Moon in 12TH EAST House This is a life when, emotionally speaking, you are closely in touch with your Unconscious mind. A good example is musician GEORGE HARRISON. Another celebrated figure with Moon in this position is BILLY GRAHAM, a genuinely more spiritual person than his public persona would suggest. In the same way, what is happening to your psyche in this life is a private, subtle and inner development that the rest of the world may not know much about.

CHAPTER TEN

Gifts and Hang-ups

In Chapter Six, FIGURING IT OUT, you were shown how to work out the East House and Node House positions for each planet, together with the various planetary aspects. This chapter will show you what they mean.

It's called GIFTS AND HANG-UPS because these are the astrological factors that determine whether you have brought any special talents, virtues or graces directly from your Key Life into your present incarnation – or whether, contrariwise, you are lumbered with difficult karma that you must try to work out of your system. This karma may take the form of neuroses, obsessions, paranoia, acute vulnerability or highly manic, disruptive inner forces threatening to break out at any minute.

You must be selective when reading the individual interpretations in this chapter. Just because you have Neptune in the 8th Node House doesn't *necessarily* mean that you died by drowning in your last life. It's a possibility, that's all – and if it sets a sensitive nerve jangling with recognition, it may well be true in your case.

Another difficulty is that you will not be able to use the sections on Mercury, Venus, Mars and Jupiter from calculations in this book alone. For reasons of space, I could not include the necessary tables for these four planets. But if you can get hold of full astrological ephemerides, or find an astrologer to work out your complete horoscope (see p. 240), you'll be able to see how these planets help your present-day personality – and why, judging by your past lives.

(To convert a Zodiac degree to a Circle No., add the degree to the far left-hand figure corresponding to the Zodiac sign in

Table 2 on p. 69. Example: 15 degrees of Scorpio. Add 15 to 210 (far left-hand figure on Scorpio line) and Circle No. = 225.)

MERCURY

The planet Mercury corresponds with the principle of communication. Anyone who is blessed by this planet has the gift of the gab, able to stitch ideas together, putting them across with verve and skill.

If Mercury forms an aspect in your horoscope, the whole business of education, learning, passing on information, writing or making speeches will play an important role in your present life, thanks to the progress that you made in your Key Life. You could have been a teacher, novelist, journalist, salesman or negotiator.

You could have influential links in your present life with a Gemini or Virgo individual.

In your Key Life you'll have been a fast-talking, quick-thinking individual, superficial rather than profound, very adaptable in out!ook and keen to try new fashions, gadgets, novelties and the iike.

If you have an *aspect with the Sun*, you will have been a relaxed personality, confident of living off your wits. But you may also have had a worrying side to your nature, which may lead to nervous troubles in this life, if you don't learn how to calm down. Example: HANS CHRISTIAN ANDERSEN.

If you have an *aspect with the Moon*, you will probably have had many lives as a writer, communicator or teacher. You'll have been an intelligent and sympathetic person – and in this life you have the gift of knowing how other people think and feel. So you have your Key Life to thank for your smooth rapport with other people's minds. Example: FEODOR DOSTOEVSKY.

If you have an *aspect to the East Point or Node*, your task in this life is to continue your quest for knowledge and your desire to spread ideas to others. You may well be picking up contacts that you had in your Key Life. At worst, you could be too restless, unable to settle down due to too wide a range of interests coming through from past lives. Example: SAMUEL GOLDWYN.

VENUS

Venus is the planet of love, beauty and tastefulness. If you have this planet strongly represented in your horoscope, you have the gift to be happy, thanks to good karma that you inherit from your Key Life.

In the past, you will almost certainly have worked in fashion, the arts, or decor or other aspects of the beauty industry. But primarily the Venusian virtues are developed not through work but social and intimate friendships: dealing with people, loving them, wanting to help them in every way you can.

In this life, you may well continue friendships with Taureans or Librans whom you knew closely in previous lives.

There is some negative karma linked to Venus. There's a danger that you may be too flippant, self-indulgent, lazy or irresponsible. On the whole, though, it brings gifts rather than hang-ups. Venus makes you a much nicer person than you would otherwise have been. Just remember, though, that to maintain this loving quality in your *future* lives, you will have to love wisely and loyally in this life.

If you have an *aspect with the Sun*, you were probably an artist in your past life – or spent your life surrounded by love, beauty and sweet-natured people. In this life, it's important that you put your talent in the arts to some creative purpose. Remember that your task is to *give* rather than take. Example: PERCY BYSSHE SHELLEY.

If you have an *aspect with the Moon*, you were probably –

though not certainly - a woman in your last life. You were a romantic, inclined to follow your heart rather than your head. This may not be a virtue in this life - beware particularly of falling in love with the wrong people, though in some cases it works out well: for example, ROBERT BROWNING.

If you have an *aspect with the East Point or Node*, your work in this life should be a continuation of artistic efforts done in the past. There is a tendency for this to make you a bit old-fashioned in your taste - indeed, you may well be drawn to work that you did in the past. Otherwise a loving, sweet and affectionate influence in your life. Example: GIUSEPPE VERDI.

MARS

Mars is the planet of vigour, power and sometimes aggressiveness. If you have this planet strongly placed in your horoscope, you tend to be energetic, direct (even blunt at times), keen to tackle new projects all the time, and quite an athletic, out-of-doors sort of individual.

In the past, you would probably - but not certainly - have been a man. Your work could have been sporty, military, organizational. You probably had command over others.

Mars is quite a troublesome planet, bringing some gifts but hang-ups as well. Its good karma is courage, warmth and initiative. You can be a real pioneer in this life, thanks to heroic efforts made in your Key Life.

But there are a number of awkward qualities attached to Mars which you may exhibit in your present life. At times you could be cruel and heartless, especially towards particular 'victims' who may have hurt you beforehand. You may have a blazing temper - gone in a second, I agree, but highly damaging at the time. Beware of hostile encounters in this life with people born under Aries.

If you have an *aspect with the Sun*, you have lots of vim and vigour. You will rarely feel tired, but may drive other people too hard. All this is due to discipline that you developed in your last life. In a second-breath life you are constantly feeling full of the joys of spring, bursting with a fresh vitality. In a life of reaction, you could be bouncing back from censorship, imprisonment and restrictions in your Key Life. Example: MARGOT FONTEYN.

If you have an *aspect with the Moon*, you have the same energy and tirelessness, but your temper will be short, your patience low, and your reflexes lightning-fast. You will certainly make a number of new enemies, and will run into some old ones, too. Your duty is to wash away this old karma by forgiveness and tolerance. But it ain't easy! Example: VASLAV NIJINSKY.

If you have an *aspect with the East Point or Node*, you have an inner drive in this life that could be a direct continuation of – or reaction to – events in your Key Life. You may be determined to revenge yourself against people who have wronged you; equally, you may be continuing energetic work that you have done many times before. Example: FRIEDRICH NIETSZCHE.

JUPITER

Jupiter is called the 'greater benefic'. In other words, it is traditionally the planet of good luck, prosperity and optimism.

If this planet is strongly represented in your horoscope, you are a born winner. Of course, at worst you can be a genial scoundrel, a wastrel or a gambler, but on the whole you should be blessed with many happy gifts – the fruits of good work in previous lives.

Humour and bonhomie are the natural attributes of the Jupiterian personality. You may have worked in your Key Life in the theatre, publishing, the law or in a job calling for much travel. But Jupiter confers gifts rather than talents: the ability to charm others, to enthuse people with wit and ideas and *joie de vivre*.

At worst, you may be too careless and slipshod, losing your place in the Dramarathon by wasting your talents on trash. You may not be entirely honest, and may evade awkward responsibilities.

It would be interesting if you found a lot of happiness in this life through contact with a Sagittarian.

If you have an *aspect with the Sun*, you are an enterprising person, perhaps getting the chance to tackle work that was denied you in an earlier life. You may be a great traveller, a person of humour and happiness. At your best, you can convey a sense of fun in life that is truly creative. At worst, you can be a saloon-bar braggart. Examples: DEBORAH KERR and SIR RICHARD BURTON.

If you have an *aspect with the Moon*, you are kindly, good-humoured, understanding and conscientious. In your previous life you will have had a friendly emotional life. In this life, you should be optimistic, thanks to a sigh of relief that old karma has been washed away. Example: BUSTER KEATON.

If you have an *aspect with the East Point or Node*, you can be like Midas, turning everything to gold! You have the happy knack of being at the right place at the right time to meet the right people. Everyone will recognize this quality of luck in your nature – but don't misuse it, or you won't see it again in a future life. Example: DAVID FROST.

SATURN

Saturn is traditionally the harsh and difficult planet. It represents everything that is grey, dull and awkward. At the same time, it has many positive virtues: responsibility, hard work, the ability to think ahead and plan sensibly.

If Saturn is strongly represented in your horoscope, your life today is not a relaxed, easy one. There's no reason why you shouldn't be happy, but it's a happiness born out of achievement and personal effort.

If you are leading a life of continuity, you'll have been a serious-minded person in the past, probably in a position of authority. This will be echoed in the pattern of your life this time. You cannot evade problems.

The same applies if this is a life of reaction. Karma – in the shape of hard times, awkward circumstances or lack of opportunity – is forcing you to mature as a soul. So this is a wonderful opportunity for you to make progress, even though you may feel the odds are stacked against you.

You may have particular contact with a Capricorn type – with quite a load of heavy karma between you.

Although Saturn can create a kind of gritty determination to do well, it also can induce quite a lot of inhibition in the personality. It also creates a guilty conscience: the ideal soap for washing karma away!

If you have an *aspect with the Sun*, you are an ambitious person, possibly with a chip on your shoulder. You are being forced to shoulder responsibilities that you have shirked in the past. You may be prone to depressions, or have one disagreeable experience that sets you back. Example: GEORGE WALLACE.

If you have an *aspect with the Moon*, you will be forced to become emotionally self-reliant, whether you like it or not. You may be denied the love you want, as a result of bad karma from the past. There could be a tricky lack of rapport with your mother – or people whom you wish to play mother towards you. Example: MARILYN MONROE.

If you have an *aspect with the East Point or Node*, you have a specially responsible role to play in your life today. You must respond positively to obligations placed on you. There could be some difficult experiences that will sorely test you, but the chance to make valuable soul-progress is great. Example: JOHN KENNEDY.

If you have a Saturn aspect, the Saturn House positions will be more significant than otherwise.

SATURN IN THE HOUSES

Saturn in 1ST NODE House Highly disciplined in Key Life. A martinet who needed to push others around, due to lack of love then. ELVIS PRESLEY.

Saturn in 1ST EAST House Determined, somewhat cold demeanour in present life. Takes life seriously, and may lack humour and joy. NIKOLAI LENIN.

Saturn in 2ND NODE House Lacked money and comforts in previous life. Could have seemed mean, through lack of funds. WOODY ALLEN.

Saturn in 2ND EAST House Likely to have money problems in this life. Possessions could be taken away from you. DORIS DAY and CHARLES LINDBURGH.

Saturn in 3RD NODE House Prevented in earlier life from thinking what you wanted – so you could revel in verbal freedom now. BERNARD SHAW.

Saturn in 3RD EAST House Concentrated mental energy in this life, but only along certain lines. Beware of nutty ideas! BERTRAND RUSSELL.

Saturn in 4TH NODE House You were deprived of family love in your past life. You have problems in present life with former mother! OSCAR WILDE.

Saturn in 4TH EAST House Some lack of family affection in this life. Feeling of independence from your nearest and dearest. MARILYN MONROE.

Saturn in 5TH NODE House Yearned for children in past life, but could have been prevented. Exaggerated love for them now? NATALIE WOOD.

Saturn in 5TH EAST House In this life, you take games too seriously! A killjoy at times, due to karma. Try to ease up, relax. HENRY KISSINGER.

Saturn in 6TH NODE House Could have been sickly in past life, or had trouble with servants, employees. PETER FALK.

Saturn in 6TH EAST House You demand efficiency from yourself and others in this life. A hypochondriac at times. BARRY GOLDWATER.

Saturn in 7TH NODE House You were disappointed in love in your last life: a failed romance, a sour marriage. MARCEL PROUST.

Saturn in 7TH EAST House Marriage may be hard at times, due to old karma with your partner which must be worked out now. ELEANOR ROOSEVELT.

Saturn in 8TH NODE House Could have been murdered in last life, with possible need to revenge yourself now. YASSAR ARRAFAT.

Saturn in 8TH EAST House You face problems in this life from someone out to get you. You must not build up yet more hate. ROBERT KENNEDY.

Saturn in 9TH NODE House You were prevented from travelling in last life – perhaps kept prisoner. Air of liberation now. BARBARA STREISAND.

Saturn in 9TH EAST House Will have some problems to do with foreigners in this life. You may be xenophobic, due to karma. STANLEY BALDWIN.

Saturn in 10TH NODE House Had big career problems/responsibilities in past. You need now to make up for lost time. SIR WINSTON CHURCHILL.

Saturn in 10TH EAST House Apt to make heavy weather of career. Over-serious about your destiny and place in world. NAPOLEON and HITLER!

Saturn in 11TH NODE House You were censored in your past life, prevented from mixing easily, perhaps expelled or exiled. OMAR SHARIF.

Saturn in 11TH EAST House You are a frustrated radical in this life, wanting to change society but thwarted by others. MARLON BRANDO.

Saturn in 12TH NODE House You could have been insensitive in last life, scoffing at more vulnerable people. PHILIP ROTH.

Saturn in 12TH EAST House You want to turn your back on religion, art, the psychic side of life – to your eventual disadvantage. INDIRA GANDHI.

URANUS

Uranus is the planet of disruption. If you have this planet strongly represented in your horoscope, you have an inner urge to do something completely new, to break up existing patterns of ideas or behaviour, and to act in a somewhat out-of-the-ordinary manner. If you do not adopt a positive attitude towards Uranus, the planet will take you over – and you'll be its victim instead of its master.

You may be getting the chance in this life to do something genuinely original. Equally, you may be getting some bad karma from your Key Life. Perhaps you were too much of a conservative, and need to be shaken up now. Perhaps you disrupted others, and are suffering the same fate at their hands now.

You could have been a creative person, a revolutionary, a radical reformer or a scientist. In this life you could have some very creative rapport with an Aquarian, renewing a contact that you've enjoyed many times in the past.

If you have an *aspect with the Sun*, you could make a unique contribution to the world's progress. You could also be a damn nuisance, upsetting the stable lives of people around you. So this can be a real gift or hang-up, whichever way you choose to play it. Example: SIGMUND FREUD.

If you have an *aspect with the Moon*, you're a highly frisky individual, independent to a fault, unable to settle easily with the same group of people. This is almost certainly a hang-up from the past. You must strive to develop loving relationships, and not be too arrogant about your own brilliance! Example: GEORGE BERNARD SHAW.

If you have an *aspect with the East Point or Node*, you have high ambitions, but may come a cropper by being too high-handed. Going your own way has its limitations, and if you cannot take other people with you, you'll fail in the end. But, like all aspects involving Uranus, it does mark you out as a special person, with special opportunities in this life. Examples: SPIRO AGNEW and INDIRA GANDHI.

If you have a Uranus aspect, this will make the following House positions that much more significant than otherwise.

URANUS IN THE HOUSES

Uranus in 1ST NODE House You were clever and inventive in last life, with a sparkling, eccentric personality. EDGAR ALLAN POE.

Uranus in 1ST EAST House In this life you can have sudden insights, clever ideas. You can go your own way and succeed. ISAAC NEWTON.

Uranus in 2ND NODE House You may have made a fortune in previous life, or had all your possessions abruptly taken away. SERGE DIAGHILEV.

Uranus in 2ND EAST House Strong desire in present life to throw aside existing lifestyle and tackle something new. ELIZABETH BARRETT BROWNING.

Uranus in 3RD NODE House You had a brilliant teacher or guru in last life, and developed unusual ideas, talents. FRANZ SCHUBERT.

Uranus in 3RD EAST House You may have a special creative skill, a revolutionary way of sowing seeds in the public's mind. PABLO PICASSO.

Uranus in 4TH NODE House Your home and family could have been disrupted in the past – or you were an unruly influence. SIR WINSTON CHURCHILL.

Uranus in 4TH EAST House You can upset people's traditional ideas. Hard for you to settle down in family atmosphere. BRIGITTE BARDOT.

Uranus in 5TH NODE House You were a creative artist/entertainer in past life – but disrupted other people's romances. YVES SAINT LAURENT.

Uranus in 5TH EAST House Highly freedom-loving in romance. Strong desire to break people's hearts. ISADORA DUNCAN and JOHN F. KENNEDY.

Uranus in 6TH NODE House You had an ingenious mind in past life. You might have stirred up trouble among work-people. ALEXANDER GRAHAM BELL.

Uranus in 6TH EAST House Might fall ill of unusual disease in this life. Quite revolutionary, changing people's working habits. MIKHAIL BAKUNIN.

Uranus in 7TH NODE House Highly disruptive in love and marriage in last life. Unable to settle into one relationship. GIACOMO CASANOVA.

Uranus in 7TH EAST House Restless in love in present life. Ambiguous feelings about marriage. Short-lived relationships. HENRY MILLER.

Uranus in 8TH NODE House Victim of sudden death in previous life. Apt to take other people's money on impulse. HENRI TOULOUSE-LAUTREC.

Uranus in 8TH EAST House You need to stir people out of their complacency. Could take sudden action against a thief. GEORGE WASHINGTON.

Uranus in 9TH NODE House May have taken unusual journey in past life, or been colonist, trader, etc among undeveloped people. JONATHAN SWIFT.

Uranus in 9TH EAST House You love new ideas, visions of the future. Could create trouble within a stable society. JULES VERNE.

Uranus in 10TH NODE House You may have helped to create great changes in previous life. An inventive, resourceful type. WILBUR WRIGHT.

Uranus in 10TH EAST House Apt to lose job, change lifestyle at short notice in your present life. MARIE ANTOINETTE.

Uranus in 11TH NODE House Full of revolutionary fervour, strong desire to change conditions in last life. FEODOR DOSTOEVSKY.

Uranus in 11TH EAST House You need to advance into the future with new technology, new social order. Have independent views. NEIL ARMSTRONG.

Uranus in 12TH NODE House You may have studied occultism in the past. May have been hurt by a secret, suddenly revealed. PAUL CÉZANNE.

Uranus in 12TH EAST House Desire to pursue inner development in this life, overthrow old and hurtful ideas. MARTIN LUTHER KING.

NEPTUNE

Neptune is the planet of illusion, fantasy and the psychic worlds. To have this planet strongly represented in your horoscope means that your conscious and unconscious minds flow together – hopefully in harmony, but not necessarily so.

With Neptune around, you are vulnerable in some way or other – vulnerable to other people but also vulnerable to your inner worries, misgivings and feelings of guilt. You can enter a world of illusion and disillusion with the dubious assistance of Neptune.

But there is a good side, too. You may well have a special psychic gift, an ability to rely on hunches and inner feelings. You may have high ideals, a continuation of training and inspiration that you will have received in your Key Life.

Work that you may have tackled in the past includes musician, dancer or painter, or something notably charitable. Less happily, you may have had a drink or drugs problem in the past, and this present life is your chance to go cold turkey.

There could be a subtle (but drifty) relationship with a Piscean in your present life.

If you have an *aspect with the Sun*, you must be true to your inner ideals, or you'll come a cropper. You may have been a priest or poet in your Key Life. There will be many temptations trying to pull you from the straight and narrow. Example: HARRY TRUMAN.

If you have an *aspect with the Moon*, you are very tender-hearted, easily fooled by appearances. But you also have the poet's touch, a definite gift from the past. At best, you have telepathy and wondrous instinct for the subtle and numinous in life. At worst, you are a fool. Example: PETER USTINOV.

If you have an *aspect with the East Point or Node*, you have a special responsibility in this present life: to inspire the people around you. You will probably be religiously-minded. There's a danger that you'll be led up the garden path by some people;

so you'll need to be very strong and sincere. Example:
ABRAHAM LINCOLN.

If you have any Neptune aspect, the following House interpretations will be that much more significant in your case.

NEPTUNE IN THE HOUSES

Neptune in 1ST NODE House You were a poet, artist, mystic in last life – or muddled soul trying to escape from life. PERCY BYSSHE SHELLEY.

Neptune in 1ST EAST House You're sensitive, poetic, fey – wrong-headed at times, but full of ideals. LEWIS CARROLL and SALVADOR DALI.

Neptune in 2ND NODE House You may have been tricked out of money, home, possessions in last life – or been a con-man! SHIRLEY TEMPLE BLACK.

Neptune in 2ND EAST House In your present life you cannot rely on word of honour, legal documents, promises – not completely. EMILY BRONTË.

Neptune in 3RD NODE House You could have been medium, dancer, musician in Key Life, but may have misused these talents. EDDIE FISHER.

Neptune in 3RD EAST House Very sensitive ability to communicate, perhaps through telepathy. May waste artistic talents. GRETA GARBO.

Neptune in 4TH NODE House Could have lost family in previous life, or had close imaginative rapport with them. W. C. FIELDS.

Neptune in 4TH EAST House You may not feel properly rooted in the everyday world. Close telepathic links with a parent. PAUL VERLAINE.

Neptune in 5TH NODE House Could have lost a child through drowning in previous life. A love-match could have slipped from grasp. SEAN CONNERY.

Neptune in 5TH EAST House You have an unreal, escapist view of romance, searching for ideal sweetheart – in your mind, at least. ELVIS PRESLEY.

Neptune in 6TH NODE House You could have been betrayed by someone in your care – a servant, pupil or patient, for instance. JOHN LE CARRÉ.

Neptune in 6TH EAST House Highly sensitive nervous system, easily thrown out by psychic upsets. High ideals in work you do. LIZA MINNELLI.

Neptune in 7TH NODE House You were let down in marriage and love last time around – or a great telepathic link then – and now? SHIRLEY MACLAINE.

Neptune in 7TH EAST House An unreal element in marriage and/or love affairs. Someone is fated to let you down, so you think. OSCAR WILDE.

Neptune in 8TH NODE House Possibly you drowned in Key Life, or drowned in alcohol. Strong links with psychic worlds. JONATHAN SWIFT.

Neptune in 8TH EAST House Possibility of death in unusual circumstances. Maybe you have a romantic attitude to death. QUEEN VICTORIA.

Neptune in 9TH NODE House A visionary in last life, possibly a traveller who never returned home. Might have been missionary. VINCENT VAN GOGH.

Neptune in 9TH EAST House Need to tell something special and ethereal to the world. Excellent for art, poetry, music. WILLIAM WORDSWORTH.

Neptune in 10TH NODE House Professional artist/mystic in last life – or disappeared through political unrest. ROD McKUEN.

Neptune in 10TH EAST House You have a mission to spread delicacy, sensitivity, inner fantasies. A bit fey yourself. PRINCESS GRACE OF MONACO.

Neptune in 11TH NODE House Could have been let down by political forces in last life. Possibly linked to religious evangelism. DAVID FROST.

Neptune in 11TH EAST House May have an unreal grasp of public opinion. Could be betrayed by large social forces. KING LOUIS XVI OF FRANCE.

Neptune in 12TH NODE House Highly delicate fantasizing ability, great links in Key Life with psychic worlds. CLAUDE MONET.

Neptune in 12TH EAST House You have marvellous access to your Unconscious. Very ethereal, sensitive, telepathic links. WOLFGANG MOZART.

PLUTO

Pluto is the most fateful planet of all. It corresponds with the dead-end life, the life of transformation, the do-or-die mission.

If you have Pluto strongly represented in your horoscope, it means that this present life marks a crucial stage in your Dramarathon. You could be facing a vital test of character, or answering for a very shabby series of actions in your Key Life.

The contribution that the Plutonian person can make in life is considerable. You seem able to summon an extra amount of energy, nerve and willpower to do what you want. On the negative side, however, you can also be quite inhuman at times, refusing to budge an inch from your stubborn viewpoint.

There could well be a special link with a Scorpio person in your present life.

If you have an *aspect with the Sun*, you are an obsessive character, taking life seriously, probing into mysteries, feeling that you have a definite mission to perform. This could be a continuation of work you have done in the past; or you may be making amends for mistakes you made in a previous life. Example: DASHIEL HAMMETT.

If you have an *aspect with the Moon*, you have a strong, insistent psyche – for good or ill. There could be a psychological problem with your mother, a hangover from your Key Life. You can be ridiculously stubborn, but able to discern the truth through great concentration. You could have irrational likes and dislikes. Examples: CARL JUNG and T. E. LAWRENCE.

If you have an *aspect with the East Point or Node*, you feel you have a special mission in life. At times you may be quite ruthless in pursuing it. If you never find it, you may have a chip on your shoulder all your life. This could be a lifetime for which you've assiduously trained for a long time in the past – or it might be the time when you turn your back on a marvellous opportunity. Examples: JOSEPH STALIN and BENITO MUSSOLINI.

If you have any Pluto aspect, the following interpretations are far more likely to be significant for you.

PLUTO IN THE HOUSES

Pluto in 1ST NODE House Last incarnation may have been dead-end life. Could have been stopped in your tracks by destiny. FRIEDRICH ENGELS.

Pluto in 1ST EAST House Strong sense of destiny in present life. You may have to go to extremes to get what you want. OLIVER CROMWELL.

Pluto in 2ND NODE House Could have lost everything in last life – been made bankrupt, homeless. Or else you were a miser. JEAN GENET.

Pluto in 2ND EAST House You may have to sacrifice your possessions. Could also be a frustrated artist, due to deep block. PRINCE CHARLES.

Pluto in 3RD NODE House You may have been imprisoned, censored, denied human rights (or physical mobility) in last life. GENE KELLY.

Pluto in 3RD EAST House Your education may be cut short, or you may be frustrated by your family. A compulsive communicator? MARY BAKER EDDY.

Pluto in 4TH NODE House You may have been denied family love in Key Life. Also could be an exile, immigrant, bad sheep. GYPSY ROSE LEE.

Pluto in 4TH EAST House Obsessive attitude towards home and family. Could be strong karmic link with mother. LIZA MINNELLI.

Pluto in 5TH NODE House Could have been romantic problems in last life. Could have been traumatic relationship with own child. FELIX MENDELSSOHN.

Pluto in 5TH EAST House Obsessive attitude towards love, leisure, sex. May have to force oneself to grow up. HELEN GURLEY BROWN.

Pluto in 6TH NODE House You may have had paranoid attitude towards servants/employees/work in previous life. LEO TOLSTOY and HENRY FORD.

Pluto in 6TH EAST House Strong sense of destiny in work or health. May be obsessive workoholic. THOMAS EDISON.

Pluto in 7TH NODE House Had traumatic marriage in last life, which may affect present prospects. Were you a recluse? HENRI TOULOUSE-LAUTREC.

Pluto in 7TH EAST House You may be obsessive about relationships. Make-or-break time(s) in love and marriage. MICKEY ROONEY.

Pluto in 8TH NODE House Could have died in difficult circumstances, or had sexual hang-ups in last life. Sense of destiny now? ISAAC ASIMOV.

Pluto in 8TH EAST House You could face danger in this life, through your own choosing (and helped by inspiration of others). CHARLES DE GAULLE.

Pluto in 9TH NODE House Could have been forcibly restricted in Key Life – so now you have an obsession to go far, learn more. JOHN GLENN.

Pluto in 9TH EAST House You have a block about travel, other nations, education – a block you must burst through. PAUL GAUGUIN.

Pluto in 10TH NODE House May have been powerful figure in Key Life, for which you must make amends now. Heavy responsibility. MOHANDAS GANDHI.

Pluto in 10TH EAST House This could be a life of destiny for you, when you make a big breakthrough – or have to start again. RICHARD NIXON.

Pluto in 11TH NODE House You could have been prevented from making your own friends or feeling as free as you'd like. MARLON BRANDO.

Pluto in 11TH EAST House You could come up against society. A tense relationship with the community. Obsessive type either pro or anti progress. THE KAISER.

Pluto in 12TH NODE House You may have said 'no' to religion and the inner worlds in Key Life – and must answer for it now. BERTRAND RUSSELL.

Pluto in 12TH EAST House You may be a frustrated priest or poet. Could be big inner worries about fate, destiny, etc. YUL BRYNNER.

CHAPTER ELEVEN

Type-casting

To conclude our astrological survey of the Dramarathon, let's do some thumb-nail analyses of public figures, just to see how the various interpretations in the last three chapters can be pulled together into a composite portrait of a soul.

To do this, I shall incorporate astrology with my own intuition, which is fallible. So don't take my words as gospel truth. All I want to do is convey an impression of how the total analysis is carried out.

ELVIS PRESLEY had Spirit in Capricorn and Moon in Pisces. It always gives a peculiar combination of strength and weakness, with even a touch of sado-masochism.

It looks as if a similar pattern could have happened in his Key Life, so his recent incarnation on Earth was a funny mixture of continuity and reaction, as though he was finding it hard to escape from a pattern that kept repeating – and reversing – itself. His 12th Node House Sun means that his Key Life was a muddled, possibly drunken existence, though he could also have been exposed to a lot of religious teaching. With his Moon in the 2nd Node House, there was also a link with comfort, money-making, and property.

Put these together, and it suggests that Elvis was an evangelical preacher in the Deep South, and made a fortune in the 19th century out of cures, salvation and anything else he could offer. Although this sounds terribly disreputable, I think that Elvis was also sincere in his beliefs – and this ambiguous attitude of make-believe sex and music, so tough and so tender, continued into his present life.

With Uranus in the 1st East House aspecting the East Point, he was likely to be a charismatic figure. Whether his life was ultimately successful, only his future life will tell.

EDWARD KENNEDY, whose horoscope has been used as an example throughout this book, has a Piscean Sun and Virgo Moon. This is quite a subdued combination of spirit and psyche for such a worshipped figure, suggesting that behind all the public relations there's a much more hesitant, worrying soul. He's got plenty of idealism, and he's capable of putting his ideals into practical effect, but there's a feeling about his horoscope that he's in danger of making himself ill through his exertions.

His House positions are fascinating. As far as the Node (past lives) Houses are concerned, the Sun's in the 12th, the Moon in the 6th – almost an exact replica of his spirit and psyche in this life. I feel sure that he has been a back-room boy (possibly in the shadow of his brothers) for quite a number of incarnations. Now he has been given the chance to prove himself.

To be honest, I feel he was an accountant, manager or clerk in his previous life. I feel there was also a connection with chemicals or oils in some way. The Kennedy brothers could have been 19th-century capitalists. Before that, there's a link with Renaissance Italy – possibly with the Vatican itself.

Teddy has a powerful Neptune, suggesting that he would suffer from his own fantasies and perhaps by being stabbed in the back. His 1st East House Sun indicates the public adoration through which he moves; and the 8th East House Moon shows the emotional background of death and misadventure that has also accompanied him.

It will be very important for him to undergo a period of retreat, silence and considerable privacy at some stage in his life. He could become much more religious than you would guess at the moment.

Another American politician, HENRY KISSINGER, has a very attractive, lightweight horoscope, suggesting that he's leading a life of continuity at the moment. His spirit is Geminian, his psyche Libran. Both signs have much in common. With Sun aspecting Mercury, Henry is at ease with ideas and their expression in speech and writing. And with his 9th Node House Sun, he has been a diplomat before. The journey he's made this life, as an immigrant from Europe to America, is similar to a journey he made in his Key Life – not from one country to another but from one faith or political system to another.

I feel Kissinger was active in 18th-century France, possibly as a cleric who became a convert of Voltaire. But he was not a revolutionary for long. Either events overtook him, or he turned quickly to the right.

I wonder whether he was an emissary from the new French Republic to the slightly older American Republic.

Finally let's look at ROGER ELLIOT, just to see whether there's anything in this Ben Jonson nonsense.

I have a Cancer spirit and Capricorn psyche, which suggests a much more conservative person than I pretend to be. I am rooted to the past, wrapped in a 'family' atmosphere and basically an emotional person who wears a tough skin at times.

This combination is echoed in the important aspects in my horoscope: a jolly, good-humoured and optimistic Jupiter, plus a more serious-minded and worrying Saturn contact to the Sun.

With this free-flowing psyche, I would guess that I was a woman in my Key Life. With the more restricted spirit, I am clearly leading a life that seeks to control and direct the psychic flow without drying it up altogether.

It's much easier for me to improvise rather than be disciplined – yet I get a guilty conscience if I'm not efficient. So I sense two strands in my Key Life: one, a dramatic woman, possibly a performer of some kind and certainly a loving person (Sun in 7th Node House), and, two, a much greyer, male, businesslike creature (Moon in 2nd Node House).

These two elements do not always live happily in my

personality. It's possible that I've had a dual series of lives, one in a boisterous, extrovert line of development, the other in a more careful, academic line – and that my present life is bringing them together.

Certainly, with Sun in the 3rd East House and Moon in the 9th, I am born to publish, promote, instruct, shout from the rooftops and generally spread the word.

Which I've done, in my own fashion, in WHO WERE YOU? I hope it enables you to think about yourself in a shrewd, sensitive and loving way. I hope you find yourself in the Dramarathon.

And, in the meantime, will the *real* Ben Jonson please own up?

CHAPTER TWELVE

Learning More

Reincarnation

To discover which of the world's great thinkers have believed in reincarnation – and why – you should read REINCARNATION: AN EAST-WEST ANTHOLOGY, compiled and edited by Joseph Head and S. L. Cranston (Quest Books, 1961). There are quotations from Apuleius to Zoroaster, including Benjamin Franklin's charming epitaph, written by himself:

> The Body of B. Franklin
> Printer,
> Like the Cover of an Old Book,
> Its Contents Torn out
> And
> Stripped of its Lettering and Gilding,
> Lies Here
> Food for Worms,
> But the Work shall not be Lost,
> For it Will as He Believed
> Appear Once More
> In a New and more Elegant Edition
> Revised and Corrected
> By the Author.

Quest Books also publish REINCARNATION: FACT OR FALLACY?, a statement by Geoffrey Hodson of the standard Theosophical view.

Much more comprehensive are THE BELIEF IN A LIFE AFTER DEATH, by C. J. Ducasse (Charles C. Thomas, 1961) and the more recent YOU CANNOT DIE, by Ian Currie (Hamlyn, 1978), which contains the most up-to-date research on out-of-the-body experiences, deathbed visions, resuscitation experiences, hypnotic regressions and mediumistic accounts of rebirth. There's also a good bibliography of out-of-the-way material.

Joan Grant's books on personal recollections of her lives include FAR MEMORY (Harper Row, 1956) and (with her husband, Denys Kelsey) MANY LIFETIMES (Doubleday).

Excellent accounts of Edgar Cayce's work – and much else besides – are in MANY MANSIONS, by Gina Cerminara (Spearman, 1967) and her other two books, THE WORLD WITHIN and MANY LIVES, MANY LOVES (Signet, 1963), all of which give friendly advice on how reincarnation and karma work in everyday life.

Astrology

The best introduction to astrology, from the lay-person's viewpoint, is undoubtedly ASTROLOGY FOR EVERYONE, by Roger Elliot (Hodder Causton, 1975, now available from Starlife at the address overleaf).

For a critical review of astrology's achievements – and failures – read RECENT ADVANCES IN NATAL ASTROLOGY, compiled by Geoffrey Dean (Analogic, 1977), soon to be followed by RECENT ADVANCES 2.

Several specialist books deal with the astrological interpretation of rebirth. D. H. Yott has written three volumes of ASTROLOGY AND REINCARNATION, while M. Schulman has written another three volumes called KARMIC ASTROLOGY. More readable and original is ASTROLOGY, KARMA AND TRANSFORMATION, by Stephen Arroyo.

Joan Hodgson's beautiful ASTROLOGY, THE SACRED SCIENCE (White Eagle Books, 1978) incorporates reincarnation and karma with astrology.

Archetypes

The most popular account of Jung's ideas is MAN AND HIS
SYMBOLS, edited by Carl G. Jung (Aldus, 1964). Also valuable
is ARCHETYPES AND THE COLLECTIVE UNCONSCIOUS, vol. 9
of Jung's Collected Works.

Your Personal Past

WHO WERE YOU? has tried to answer an intimate question
in a public way. Inevitably it can have given you only a
generalized reply.

   If you would like to know more about your personal
Dramarathon, as revealed in your birth-chart, you can contact
me by writing to Starlife, Cossington, Bridgwater, Somerset,
England, enclosing a stamped addressed envelope. I shall send
you full details of how I can help you.